HALTON

NEW YORK TIMES AND USA TODAY BESTSELLING AUTHOR
MELANIE MORELAND

Halton - Vested Interest #6 by Melanie Moreland
Copyright © 2019 Moreland Books Inc.
Registration # 1160058
Ebook ISBN # 978-1-988610-23-8
Print book ISBN # 978-1-988610-22-1

MORELAND BOOKS INC.

Edited by Lisa Hollett—Silently Correcting Your Grammar

Cover design by Melissa Ringuette, Monark Design Services

Formatting by Vellum

DEDICATION

For my readers who asked
And Melissa
This one is for you.
Thank you.

Eternal~E

ONE

Halton

"Tell your client he has twelve hours to decide."

There was a pause on the phone.

"Did you hear me?" I snapped.

"It's nine p.m., Hal. You expect him to decide tonight?"

"This is his fucking kid. If he's really the parent he insists he is, the decision will take five minutes."

I slammed down the phone, spinning my chair so I faced the window. I drew in some much-needed oxygen. Long, steady breaths that would calm and center me.

It didn't help.

I reached toward the sideboard and poured a splash of scotch into the crystal tumbler. Briefly, I held the glass to the light, admiring the golden hue, then I tossed back the liquor. The burn in my throat felt good, the rich smoothness of the scotch coating my taste buds and warming my chest. I poured another shot and sat back, staring into the night.

The early autumn evening was clear. The lights of the city shone brightly all around me. Up on the fortieth floor, in the corner office, I had a clear view of Toronto harbor and the city. I often stared out the window as I reflected on my day or mulled over the best solution to a problem.

Or cursed deadbeat parents who felt they deserved to be part of their kid's life on a whim.

With a sigh, I leaned my head back into the thick leather of my office chair and sipped my scotch as I tugged my tie loose.

This case was pissing me off to no end. A divorced couple—the mother retaining full custody, while the father did the usual every second weekend and occasional evening visitation.

When it suited him—which wasn't often.

As my client, his ex-wife, had proven, he was a no-show more than he kept his word. Until she met someone else who stepped up to the plate and became a father figure to her daughter and a partner to her.

Now this jackass wanted to be a part of his daughter's life and was demanding more visitation, insisting that his ex-wife had kept his daughter away from him and poisoned her mind against him.

Luckily, my client kept impeccable records on missed visitation, all the texts and emails she had sent to remind him of upcoming birthdays, important dates, and visiting times. All of which he ignored until he found out he was being replaced.

And the kicker was how generous my client was being. Rather than put her daughter through a custody battle that could get ugly, she was trying to find a solution. Her offer of steady visitation was more than fair, especially given the fact that he was doing this because his nose was out of joint. His ego wouldn't allow him to be replaced. And while Janet knew that, she still gave him the benefit of the doubt.

"I don't want Kimberly not to know her father," she explained to me. "He was a good dad when we were together, and she adored him."

"That was then," I argued. I wanted to go after him, no holds barred, and have him erased from their lives completely. "His track record speaks for itself."

She looked sad. "I know, but I'm hoping if I make the offer, he'll try. Really try. So, if Kimmy ever asks me why, I can tell her honestly how hard I attempted to have him be part of her life." She sighed, looking past me to the window. "George loves her too, but Hank is her father." She lifted her shoulders in a resigned shrug. "As George says, no child can have too much love. If she can have both of them, then it's a good thing."

Her words still echoed in my head. *No child can have too much love.*

Some kids had no love. Sometimes they were pawns—caught in a game they never asked to play.

A game where they were the losers—every time.

I shook my head to clear my thoughts, locking up the memories, pushing away the feelings where they belonged.

In the past.

The door opening behind me startled me, and I spoke without turning around.

"Why are you still here?"

A long sigh met my ears. "Because my tyrant of a boss is still here, so like the good soldier I am, I stayed."

I turned and met the steady gaze of my assistant.

"Now you're a soldier?"

Rene's eyes crinkled as he chuckled. Twenty years my senior, he had more energy than I did most days. He had been married young, and his son was my age, married with two kids Rene doted on. His wife had passed away ten years prior, and since then he was a self-declared ladies' man. Tall, thin, with café-au-lait colored skin and a polished bald head, he was dressed in his usual flamboyant style. It had taken me a while to get used to his wardrobe. If it had been a large law office, he would have stuck out like a sore thumb, but since it was my own practice, I allowed it.

Dark dress pants, a brilliant blue shirt, a wild vest, and a jaunty tie was his idea of an office uniform. Other days, his patterned jackets and pocket squares were vivid and bright. The funkiest shoes always adorned his feet. A gold earring gleamed in his ear. His wardrobe screamed uptown, but his work was definitely downtown, and I'd be lost without him. He ran my office with precision and put up with my grueling schedule without a complaint.

"I'm sure I have the outfit to prove it."

I smirked. "No doubt."

He set a pile of folders on my desk. "I've updated your calendar, made sure all your research was up to date, returned all your messages, and answered all the emails I could. I also rescheduled your dinner with the flavor of the month until Thursday. You have a new client meeting Wednesday evening, and I know how pissy Ms. Molly gets when you keep her waiting."

My lips quirked. "Good thinking."

"She bothers me."

I tried not to laugh. "Does she now? In what way?"

"Her attitude. She's a handful. Don't get me started on that voice either. Like nails on a chalkboard."

"Thanks for the heads-up."

"I'm telling you, when you end it—and we both know you will—she's gonna take it badly. She's a clinger."

"Duly noted."

"You need to find a nice girl. Settle down. Stop this casual shit."

"Not interested, thanks."

He studied me, crossing his arms. "You have a lot to offer someone, Halton."

I snorted. "Sex-wise, maybe. That's all I'm interested in."

"It's all you allow yourself to be interested in."

I waved my hand dismissing his words. "It's no skin off your nose, Rene. Back off."

"It would make my life easier, not having to remember who is who and with whom you're sleeping this week."

"I pay you well enough to keep track of those details. Do your job."

"I do it well, thank you very much."

I lifted one shoulder. "Meh. I guess."

"Oh, don't fall over yourself with the compliments," Rene snipped. "I'd like to see someone else put up with your broody ass the way I do."

He was right and we both knew it, but I liked to give him a hard time. He certainly gave me one every chance he got.

I sat back in my chair and pursed my lips.

"Why do you work for me if I'm such a miserable bastard?"

"Because you wear a suit like no one's business and it makes my nether regions sing when I watch you strut around," he deadpanned.

I blinked. "I have no idea how to respond to that."

Rene rolled his eyes and became serious. "I work for you because of what you do, Halton."

I interrupted him with an impatient wave of my hand. "Stop calling me that. You know I prefer Hal."

He shook his head. "*Hal* is your persona. He is the asshole other attorneys and judges have to deal with every day. The man who refuses to back down from an argument. The individual who presents an indifferent persona to the world. I know the real Halton. The man who fights on behalf of children. For the woman trying to leave her abusive husband. For the dad who would be a better parent for his child. You battle for the underdog."

"Keep the overflowing heart stuff to yourself. I like to see justice done. Simple. And I like to win."

Rene turned on his heel and headed to the door. "Say whatever you want. Underneath all that bluster and snarky attitude is a good man."

"Get out of my office."

Rene paused with a smirk. "Don't worry, boss man. I like my job too much. I'll keep that part to myself."

"Do that."

He shut the door and my phone rang.

Seeing the number, I smirked. "Hal Smithers," I barked into the phone.

"We'll accept the deal."

"I'll let my client know."

I hung up and picked up my scotch.

Victory.

TWO

Halton

"You're not paying attention," Molly snapped.

I glanced up from my phone with a frown. "I told you I was in the middle of an important case. My work takes priority. I was very clear from the onset of this...whatever you want to call it, with you."

She sniffed. "I thought it was a relationship."

With a sigh, I set down my phone and picked up my scotch, sipping the golden liquid with appreciation. I studied Molly in the dim light of the restaurant. She was lovely—if you were into tall, willowy brunettes with great tits.

Which I was.

But her expression was dissatisfied. Her dark eyes narrowed as she tapped her wineglass with her long nails and regarded me with a scowl pulling down her mouth. I was tempted to remind her frowning causes wrinkles, but I refrained.

"I don't do relationships, Molly. I was very upfront about that. I'm happy to take you to dinner or the odd social function, even away for the weekend, but that's all I can offer you."

"And sex," she added. "You like sex."

"Yep. I was upfront about that too. You've never complained about it before." I paused, choosing my words carefully. "I'm not your happily ever after, Molly. I don't do that shit. You know that."

"You are the most emotionally unavailable man I have ever met."

I wanted to roll my eyes. This was hardly news. I didn't believe in emotions—unless it was anger that I could funnel into winning a case. Fury, frustration, hate—those emotions were useful to me. They were what I built my business on. And they were more truthful than the

6

one emotion I steered clear of. *Love*. It was the most dangerous one of them all. Four small letters that had the power to destroy everything in their path.

I shook my head to clear my train of thought. Molly was frowning again, obviously pissed off that I wasn't responding to her words. I picked up my drink again.

I had a feeling I would need it tonight.

"I think if you look hard enough, none of us males are very invested, Molly. At least not the kind of man you seem to like."

"What does that mean?" She crossed her arms, pressing her already high breasts together, making them even more visible.

"You like rich men. Men like me who buy you things. Take you to dinner."

She tossed her hair. "And?"

I shrugged. "The kind of man who can afford *you* isn't usually looking for an in-depth relationship."

"You are so rude."

"I call it as I see it. Besides, you knew all this going in. I take you to dinner, we have sex, I buy you the occasional present. It's worked so far, so what's the problem?"

She sat back, crossing her legs, showing off her calves in her short skirt. Her top leg swung quickly, showing her agitation.

"I've barely seen you for two weeks. And why do you look so tired? The bags under your eyes are worse than normal. It's not attractive, Hal."

I refrained from telling her exactly how hard I worked—it was a concept too foreign for her to understand. So was my constant insomnia. She wouldn't know about it since I never spent the night with her—or anyone. I kept that stuff private. Instead, I held up my phone. "Work. I'm juggling five cases right now, all of them nasty. I pushed everything aside to have dinner with you tonight."

"And you've been on your phone the whole time," she whined. Her voice grated on my nerves, and I recalled Rene's comments. He was right—it was nasal and high, yet somehow, I had never noticed it until now. I studied her a little harder. I also never noticed how much makeup she wore or her rather questionable wardrobe choices. If she bent over the table, I was certain the restaurant was going to get quite the show. Her tits practically hung out of the plunging neckline. Between that and the inappropriate skirt length, she screamed "Look at me!"

What had I been thinking?

Internally, I shook my head. As usual when it came to women, I hadn't been thinking with the right head. Those great tits had clouded my judgment and led me astray once again.

"I need more attention," she added. "I want to go away this weekend." She lifted her chin. "And I want a present to make up for the time you've been ignoring me."

I was done. With a sigh, I set down my glass—it was a shame we hadn't eaten yet. I was looking forward to my filet. I lowered my voice, using the one I had honed over the years of talking to judges, juries, and clients. It cajoled and soothed, led them in the direction I needed them to go.

"I think what we need is to call this dinner what it really is, sweetheart. Our last meal together. A goodbye."

I called all the women I dated sweetheart. It saved my ass trying to make sure I called out the right name during sex.

Her eyebrows flew up. "*What?*"

"We want two different things," I stated, then launched into my usual exit summary. "You're great, Molly, and you deserve a guy who can appreciate all you have to offer. Who can devote his time and attention to you. That's not me. I don't think we should see each other anymore."

"You're breaking up with me?"

"Yes."

Her fingers tightened on her wineglass, and I could read her thoughts.

"I wouldn't do that." I indicated the wineglass she was slowly lifting. "My scotch would burn far more going in your direction."

"You wouldn't," she gasped quietly. She eyed me warily, unsure if she believed her own words.

She was right. I would never throw liquor in the face of a woman, no matter what she had done. I had class and manners.

And I wouldn't want to waste the scotch.

"Try me," I taunted.

"You're an asshole."

"Guilty as charged."

Her fingers moved again, and I waited, cursing the fact that I had worn my favorite gray suit today. The red wine was gonna stain it for sure.

Dammit.

Then, in a move I didn't expect, she picked up her water glass and flung the contents at me. I tilted my head, and thankfully, her aim was awful and most of the cold liquid flew past my shoulder, hitting the wall behind me, the sound loud in the quiet restaurant, the ice hitting the surface and the water running in rivulets to the carpet.

She stood, screeching at me.

"No one breaks up with me!"

I lifted my napkin and wiped at my cheek.

"I think, sweetheart, you're wrong there. I just did."

She stamped her foot like a toddler and stormed out of the restaurant, cursing my name in a very unladylike fashion.

I had to admit, this was a first for me. Usually I broke up with them in private and sent flowers the next day wishing them well. Molly had been an exception from the moment I met her. A mistake —a huge error in judgment on my part.

A waiter appeared, removing her table setting. Another waiter made quick work of the mess she had made behind me. "Another scotch, sir?"

I was going to refuse and ask for the bill, but to my surprise, after the initial gawking, everyone around me went back to their meals, not in the least put out.

I was sure I should be more embarrassed than I was, yet I felt only relief. A scene was a small price to pay to be rid of her. I had realized as soon as the words were out of my mouth, I was ready for her to be gone. She was tiresome and taxing. Constantly at me over every detail in her life—most of which I had no interest in. Demanding gifts—of the kind that came in a box and that of my time. The kind I could buy were easier to give, but my time was limited, and I was over it. All of it. I needed to take a break from women completely and concentrate on my career.

"Yes, please. I'd like my dinner as soon as possible. I'm starving. Bring me her salad as well. I'll eat it all."

He nodded sagely. "Very good, sir."

I picked up my phone, grateful the water hadn't hit it. I would be lost without it. It was as necessary to me as breathing these days. I smirked wryly—I was glad she had chosen the water. I had a feeling red wine would have stung as well if she had been lucky enough to have hit me with it.

I went back to my emails, thankful for the distraction.

At least I wouldn't have to send her flowers. But I was going to block her number from my phone and instruct Rene I was no longer taking her calls and she wasn't welcome in the office.

He was going to laugh gleefully when I told him.

Bastard.

THREE

Halton

I strode through the door, past Rene, and into my private office, slamming the door closed. I flung my briefcase on the sofa and sat down heavily, resting my head back on the cool leather. It felt good against the anger-flushed skin on my neck. Words from the case this morning echoed in my head.

"But your honor, it's not in the best interest of the child!" I argued, knowing my words would fall on deaf ears but determined to try.

Judge Sparks lifted one eyebrow in my direction, her voice filled with derision. "I'll decide what is in the best interest of the child, counselor."

"It's not the mother," I spat. I indicated my client, sitting beside me, his shoulders slumped. "Her father has great concern about her mother's influence on her. He doesn't wish to deny her visitation, but he feels it would be best if he were the primary caregiver for her."

The judge shook her head. "I disagree. I believe the child belongs with her mother. Your client gets visitation. I suggest he make the best use of it."

The gavel was loud in the courtroom, announcing the end of the case and her exit. I met Eric's disappointed gaze.

"We can appeal. Try for a different judge." I hated getting Judge Sparks. She always sided with the mother. Add in the snake of a lawyer Eric's wife had retained and the decision hadn't shocked me, but I had hoped things would be different.

He shook his head. "I can't put Maddy through more, Hal." He sighed. "We've tried everything." He glanced over to where his ex-wife stood, talking to the other lawyer, the glow of victory evident on her face. "All I can hope is she tires of the responsibility fast. That once she feels I've been punished enough, she'll let me have Maddy," he added, studying his ex-wife. "I can hope for that, and in the meantime, be there when Maddy needs me and try to undo the negative influence Audrey has on her."

I followed his worried gaze. His ex-wife was a nutjob. Much too focused on keeping her daughter skinny and making sure she hung with the "right kids," rather than allowing her to be a little girl. She treated Maddy like a friend instead of a child, using her eight-year-old as a sounding board for her problems. Nothing was ever right for Audrey, and she complained endlessly.

Her constant criticism had driven Eric away, and he had fought to keep Maddy, hating the way his ex-wife made Maddy feel and act. I had personally seen how her mother affected her. She became withdrawn and nervous with her mother, always quiet and proper, the light gone from her eyes. She assumed the mantle of her mother's sadness, acting as if it were her own. But with Eric, she was happy and loved. She laughed and played—got dirty and asked for hugs. He put no expectations on her aside from being a little girl. That was what she needed. To be loved unconditionally. Not to be treated like a mini adult and carrying the weight of the world on her shoulders.

But her mother's lawyer had spun everything. Used the guilt Maddy felt to make sure she asked to stay with her mother. Somehow got the judge he wanted. Produced affidavits from friends and colleagues saying how close Maddy and Audrey were. I had no idea how her lawyer, Scott Hutchings, had so many people lie for her, but he did. He did it all the time. He was my nemesis, and I hated everything he stood for.

Which basically was that winning was everything—no matter what you had to do to achieve it.

No matter whose life you screwed up.

The sound of my door opening brought me out of my musings. Rene entered, carrying a tray. He slid it onto the low table in front of me.

"I brought you coffee and a sandwich. Eat, dwell, then shake it off. You did everything you could, Halton. I know it. You know it. Your client knows it. At least you got more visitation than they were offering and stricter rules in place about co-parenting."

I sighed, accepting the steaming mug he was holding out for me. "I know. Eric thinks she'll slip back into her old ways of finding Maddy more trouble than she's worth. I told him to keep records, emails, texts, and to tape all their phone calls."

"Then we'll let her self-combust. Eric will keep an eye on his child. He loves her too much not to." He paused. "And you have other clients who need you."

"I know. One of them is against Hutchings again. I hate that lowlife. He's the sort that gives us lawyers a bad rap."

Rene slid a folder onto the table. "I found some information that should help on that case. The father's been giving into his love for gambling. He dipped into the savings they had for their son's college fund."

I whistled. "He was on thin ice already—even with Hutchings on his case."

Rene chuckled. "I know. Amy hadn't even looked at that account. I noticed the discrepancy and asked her to get me the records. I got the contact Reid Matthews put us in touch with to do some digging as well." He tapped the folder. "Wyatt found some interesting things."

"Excellent. Reid did us a solid, finding him. If I can't have the master, one of his disciples is a great replacement."

Rene laughed. I had used Reid a couple of times for special cases. The brilliant genius IT man for my friend Bentley's company BAM, Reid had been invaluable.

And totally loyal to Bentley, no matter how much I offered him to come to my firm. Finally, he had recommended a friend of his, who was almost as good as Reid. He was great coming up with information I could use in cases. Even things I couldn't use but helped steer me down a more legal avenue. His one stipulation was he worked from home—he hated everything that smacked of "the man" and the corporate world.

Except the large retainer I paid him. That, he accepted happily, and I had to respect his honesty. He hadn't let me down, and I was glad to have his services.

Especially when up against someone as dirty as Scott Hutchings.

I sighed and rubbed my eyes.

"Are you not sleeping at all?" Rene asked.

I waved my hand, not wanting to get into it with him. "I'm fine."

He waited, pinning me with his stern gaze.

"Fine," I acquiesced. "The insomnia is worse right now."

"You really need to see someone about that, Halton."

I shook my head. "Nothing has worked. Ever. A couple of hours of broken sleep seem to be all I get most nights. If that."

"It doesn't look like you're getting even that much."

He was right, but I wasn't going to tell him. Fifteen- or twenty-minute naps off and on were all I was able to get these days. I was exhausted.

He opened his mouth to talk, and I held up my hand. "I'll try the medication again if I can't break the cycle soon."

His mouth tightened, but he remained silent. Rene knew how much I hated taking medication and, even worse, how the side effects made me feel. But I was getting desperate enough to deal with the sluggishness that lingered. It might be better than the exhaustion, but I still resisted.

He pushed the tray closer, walked to the door, and paused. "You need to take better care of yourself."

I had no fast retort to shout after him. I knew he was probably right, but I had no idea how to do a better job.

I picked up my sandwich, taking a bite.

I thought about what he'd said regarding the case. He was right. I'd done all I could for Eric. I could only hope his knowledge of the way his wife worked held true and, in a short time, Maddy would be back with him on a more permanent basis. I would go back to court to fight for the legal documents to make it forever.

I flipped open the file Rene handed me, determined this time my client would win out. I took the losses hard, because, to me, they were personal.

Every single case.

I rubbed my tired eyes, glancing toward the clock. I wasn't surprised to see it was past nine. Darkness had descended outside, the only light in my office the reading lamp behind me. My lined notepad was filled with my "chicken scratch," as Rene called it. Wyatt had found a lot of bad behavior from my client's soon-to-be ex-husband, some of which would help disprove his side of the story and give any judge pause before granting him anything but supervised visitation.

I stood, grabbing a bottle of water from the fridge and sipping it as I stared out the window and thinking.

I only took cases I believed in. I fought for embattled spouses, kids too little to have their voices heard, teenagers being screwed by the system. I dug and searched until I was certain my clients were on the up-and-up, refusing to represent anyone I felt was lying. You lied to me, and that was it. I removed myself from the case. The truth, I could handle, work with, figure out how to let it do the least amount of damage if it was bad. A lie ended it all. I had learned early in life how lies could destroy a person.

There were no second chances with me—ever.

My stomach rumbled, interrupting my musings. I grabbed my coat, leaving my office the way it was. No one would enter without my permission. Not even the cleaners. They only came in when

Rene was there to oversee them. I was too particular, and I didn't like people in the office when it was empty. It was one of my quirks.

One of many, Rene would say.

I hurried across the street, the wind biting into my skin. The temperature had dropped, and rain was starting to fall. Autumn rain —the kind that dampened your clothes and got under your skin no matter what you were wearing. I shivered as I stepped into the neighborhood bar. I shrugged out of my coat, shaking it to get off some of the moisture, then headed toward the corner and my favorite booth. The bar was surprisingly empty for a Friday night and I was grateful. I ordered a half pint of Guinness on tap and one of their house-made burgers. I needed the meat and carbs. I hadn't eaten anything except the sandwich, and that had been hours ago.

I settled against the worn bench, the padding on the seat thin, and scarred wood carved deep with various initials, dates, and hearts of loves long dead. I scrolled through my phone, switching profiles to my personal one. There were a few emails from advertisers, which I deleted. A couple of personal ones from friends inquiring about dinner or a show, which I quickly replied to as having to take a rain check, and finally, one from my mother.

I paused, my thumb hovering over the banner, unsure if I wanted to read the message now, wait until later, or delete it without even reading. I had come over to the bar to decompress and relax. An email from my mother would probably have the opposite effect on me.

I set down the phone and picked up my Guinness, taking a long sip. My gaze wandered, and I caught the eyes of a woman sitting at the bar. Her scrutiny never wavered, meeting my eyes steadily.

Bright silver and gray hair brushed past her shoulders in waves, hanging loosely around a pretty face. Glasses were perched on the end of her nose, giving her an impish look. Judging from her proximity to the bar, she was short. She wore a blue coat, draped over her shoulders as if to ward off the chill. In front of her was a Guinness —the same as mine. She lifted it in a silent toast, and with a smirk, I lifted my glass, then picked up my phone again. I had no interest in a cougar—even a highly attractive one. I glanced up quickly again—she looked familiar, but I couldn't place her. My burger arrived, and I deleted my mother's message without reading it and dismissed the thoughts of the pretty woman at the bar. I was hungry.

I switched profiles, checking my business one, knowing anything important would have been handled earlier by Rene. So, it was more to catch up from what had happened during the day and see if anything new had come in that I had to look at.

I scrolled as I ate. The thick burger oozed cheese and bacon, satisfying my hunger. I polished off the salad and fries, then pushed away my plate and ordered another small beer. While I was waiting, I finished my messages.

A Guinness slid in front of me, and I glanced up to say thanks. My eyes widened at the sight of the woman I had noticed at the bar, now standing by my table, her hand lingering on the glass she had placed in front of me.

"Is liquor the best way of getting your attention?" she asked.

Her voice was soft, lyrical almost in its quality. It was pleasant.

I shook my head. "My attention is focused on business right now, sorry."

She slid into the booth opposite me. "Excellent. I was hoping you'd say that."

I leaned back, studying her, shocked to realize she wasn't an older woman at all. Despite the silver and gray hair, her face was youthful. She was younger than my thirty-six years—closer to thirty, I estimated. Her skin was ivory, with light color in her cheeks—from the alcohol or embarrassment, I didn't know. Without her glasses on, her eyes were a verdant green—bright and clear against the color of her hair and skin. She wasn't tall—below average I guessed, having not seen how high the heels were she had on her feet. She was delicate-looking—almost too thin in my opinion. Yet something about her gaze and the curve of her mouth hinted at intelligence, wit, and strength below the surface.

I sighed. "Listen, sweetheart. I'm flattered but not in the market right now." I rubbed the back of my neck. "It's been a long week, and I just came in for a quiet beer and a bite to eat."

The color in her cheeks deepened, but she refused to back down. "My, what an ego you have. Do all women you see hit on you?"

I shrugged. "Usually."

She laughed quietly, pulling the coat tight around her shoulders. "I'm not here to proposition you, Mr. Smithers."

I lifted one eyebrow in challenge. "You have me at a disadvantage. You know who I am, but I don't know you."

She held out her hand. It was small, easily encompassed by my much larger one. "Fiona."

"Nice to meet you, Fiona. May I be honest here?"

Her face hardened. "I prefer honest, Mr. Smithers."

"Since you assure me you're not here to proposition me, I'm not sure what you want or need, but tonight isn't the night to ask me for it." I slid a card across the table toward her. "If you're looking for a donation to some charity, there's a link on my site to direct you. If you're a reporter, I don't talk about my cases. If you have a legal issue, I suggest you call my office at the number on the card, and I'll get back to you as soon as I can. Frankly, it will be a while because my caseload is full up. Tell my assistant what you need, he'll pass it along, and I'll recommend someone for you."

"I'm not after money or an interview. I need a lawyer. I don't want someone else. I want—I *need*—your services."

I felt a flare of anger. I was tired. The week had been a difficult one, and I had a long weekend ahead of me of more work. I was slammed with cases and had decided a few weeks ago not to take on any new ones unless they were an emergency. Rene and I discussed any new prospective clients, and then we matched them up with other good, honorable attorneys I trusted, if possible. I couldn't remember him mentioning anyone named Fiona, so I doubted she had even tried to get in contact. She was simply taking the short route, and it pissed me off to no end.

I stood, flinging some money on the table and leaving the untouched beer. "As I said, get in touch with my assistant."

I strode from the bar, not bothering to look behind me. I headed across the street, deciding to call it a night and head home. I walked down the ramp of the parking garage toward my car, muttering under my breath about pushy women when I heard it.

Running feet behind me.

I pivoted. Fiona was racing across the parking lot, headed my way. She stopped in front of me, her breath coming out fast. She was short—at least a foot shorter than my 6'2". Her hair, damp from the rain, clung to her head, and she was clutching her coat.

"Please," she gasped. "I didn't mean to upset you, Mr. Smithers. I simply didn't know what else to do. I waited outside your office all night watching for you to come out."

I ran a hand through my hair, my anger dispersing at her genuine distress. Up close, I could see the exhaustion on her face, the signs of sleepless nights and worry, all too familiar, that were etched into her skin.

"Call my office on Monday, Fiona," I said, my voice calmer. "Tell Rene I said to fit you in." I could at least listen to her.

She shook her head. "I tried that. Your pit-bull assistant won't let me past him."

Her description of Rene was accurate, but I frowned. Rene never made the judgment call. That was my responsibility.

"I'm sorry, I don't understand. You've called?"

"Yes. I came to the office as well. He told me your caseload was full and you weren't interested in speaking to me."

Something about her voice caught my attention. That feeling of familiarity hit me again.

"Have we met?" I asked.

"Once," she replied. "It wasn't exactly, ah, comfortable."

"Oh?"

"I was with my husband. The man divorcing me now. The man I need your help to fight against."

A memory tickled the edges of my brain. A dinner a couple of years prior. A roomful of lawyers.

One in particular.

I narrowed my eyes. "Who is your husband?"

She shivered. "Scott Hutchings."

FOUR

Halton

After she dropped that bombshell, we stood, our eyes locked in the parking lot.

Now I knew why she looked so familiar.

"Nice try, Mrs. Hutchings. Whatever game you and your husband are playing—I'm not interested."

I turned to walk away, but she grabbed my arm. "Please, Mr. Smithers! I'm not playing a game."

I pivoted, shaking off her hold. She met my furious gaze, honesty leaking from her eyes.

"Scott wants a divorce. He ended our marriage, Mr. Smithers. Please, help me."

"Why me? There are lots of other lawyers in town. Get one of them."

"No, I want you."

"Why?"

"Because you hate Scott almost as much as I do, and I know you'll do a good job."

Her statement startled me.

"Hate is a strong sentiment."

"It's how I feel—finally."

I studied her. "I'm going to check out your story."

She lifted her chin. "Unlike Scott, I have nothing to hide." A long shiver ran through her body, and I remembered her earlier words.

"I waited outside your office all night watching for you to come out."

It had been getting colder all evening, and the rain had started hours ago. The building was locked at six.

21

"Where did you wait for me?" I asked, curious.

"In the doorway across the street so I could see if you came out. Or if your car did."

"Did you plan to jump in front of my car?"

"If need be." Another shiver raced through her.

I glanced around the almost empty parking lot. "Where did you park?"

She shook her head. "I don't have a car. I took the bus."

I made a decision and grasped her elbow. "Come with me."

"Where are we going?"

"I'll drive you home."

"But my case—"

I interrupted her with a shake of my head. "Mrs. Hutchings, I don't conduct my business in the late hours of a Friday night in a parking lot while a potential client freezes to death. I'll drive you home, and you can come into the office on Monday and we'll talk."

The auto unlock feature of the remote in my pocket clicked, and I opened the passenger door, indicating she should get inside. Once she slid in, I closed the door and walked around to the driver's side, my head swimming.

I hadn't heard anything about Hutchings's marriage failing. Not a whisper. Until I had confirmation, I was going to proceed with caution. But I wouldn't leave a woman stranded and freezing, even if she was the wife of someone I disliked.

I recalled meeting Fiona Hutchings at a dinner I had attended. Scott had been there, drinking too much and talking too loud, the same way he did in a courtroom. He loved calling attention to himself. He was a braggart and a liar, and it was all I could do not to tell him to shut up.

We had been seated at the same table, and I ended up across from him, barely able to stand the fact that I was being subjected to his company. Somehow Fiona ended up beside me and at first I hadn't known she was his wife. She had only introduced herself by her first name, and we spoke briefly. She was elegant and classy, her hair—

blonder then—swept into a knot at the base of her neck, her dress demure. I remember thinking her charming and witty for the few moments we conversed. Although she wasn't my usual type, I also found her attractive. Then I saw the thin wedding band on her finger, and I reined myself in—I never got involved with married women. It was another one of my rules. Be it someone I met at a bar, one of these dinners, or especially clients—if you were married, it was hands off.

The next moment, Scott's voice boomed across the table, so deep it was almost a snarl.

"Fiona! Breaking bread with the enemy now, are you?"

She had flushed, and I realized to whom she was married and tried not to shudder. So much for first impressions.

Another attorney at the table chuckled. "Now, now, Scott. This is social. When we're out of the courtroom, we can all get along, right?"

Scott's expression said it all, even though he laughed along with everyone else, but he insisted she switch seats. He made a great show of flinging his arm around her shoulders and kissing her. I was certain at the time she had turned her head slightly, so the kiss fell on her cheek rather than her mouth. I studiously ignored Scott the rest of the evening, although I found my glance fixated on Fiona on occasion.

She spoke little to anyone else and seemed uncomfortable and anxious, as if she felt out of her depth. On occasion, a pained looked crossed her face, and I wondered if Scott's behavior embarrassed her. I recall thinking she looked out of place beside him—almost too gentle to be associated with him. I wondered then how she could stand to live with someone so unscrupulous—unless she was cut from the same cloth. I knew all too well that appearances could be deceiving. She might come across as sweet, but she could be a coldhearted bitch for all I knew, using the veneer of her softness to her advantage. Wit and charm covered a multitude of sins.

Yet, the woman who had beseeched me a few moments ago—the woman who stood in the cold for hours desperate to talk to me, didn't seem like a coldhearted bitch. Something in the depths of her tormented green eyes, in the pleading tone of her voice, told me she was honest.

I slid into the car and pushed the button to start the engine, setting the heat high on her side.

"It'll be warm in a moment," I assured her.

"Thank you."

"Where do you live?"

"If you could drop me at the subway, that would be fine."

I sighed as I clipped my seat belt in place. "It's raining harder now. I'll drive you home. Give me the address."

"Mississauga, Mr. Smithers. It's a long drive for you. If you drop me at the subway, that would be fine. My, ah, *room* is a couple of blocks from the stop on the other end."

"Room?" I asked, confused. Why was she in a room? And why was she out in Mississauga?

Hutchings, as I recalled, lived in a ritzy area of Toronto.

"I went there after Scott—" she swallowed "—after things ended." She glanced out the window, not meeting my gaze. "I'm staying with a friend."

"Have you been in contact with him?"

She turned her head, the pain in her eyes evident. "No. He hasn't returned my calls except to say he is going to cancel my cell phone plan and not pay for it anymore. He kicked me out, Mr. Smithers. Ended our marriage, handed me some money, and drove me to a hotel. He barely gave me time to pack a bag—it was as if he couldn't stand to be around me anymore. He took away my keys to the house. I was in shock, and I had nowhere else to go, so I'm grateful for Joanne's generosity."

For a moment, there was only the purr of the engine and the low hum of the fan in the car as I processed her words.

Whatever had happened, whatever occurred, if she was telling the truth, Scott Hutchings was a complete bastard to his wife. I wasn't the least bit shocked to discover that, but I wanted the whole story.

My fingers tightened on the steering wheel.

"Hal," I informed her.

"I'm sorry?"

"I prefer my clients to call me Hal. Not Mr. Smithers."

"Am I your client now?"

"Come see me on Monday, and we'll decide."

Monday morning, I was already in the office when Rene arrived. Today, he was dressed entirely in black, but his vest was a swirl of color, like bright starbursts in the night. A bow tie completed the outfit. His bald head gleamed.

I shook my head. "Did you wax your head? Jesus, you're going to blind me today."

He laughed, smoothing his hand over his skull. "The ladies dig it."

I let his words pass. I wasn't in the mood to hear stories about his personal life.

He set a coffee on my desk. "You're here early. Still no sleep?"

Ignoring his question, I indicated the chair in front of me. "I need to talk to you."

Frowning, he sat. "That sounds ominous."

"Fiona Hutchings."

His eyebrows rose. "What of her?"

"Why didn't you tell me she had been calling?"

"Because she refused to tell me why she was calling. She's Scott's wife, and you loathe that man. I couldn't think of any reason you would want to talk to her. I assumed it was for one of the many charities the various wives in the legal field are involved in. I told her to send a letter."

I shook my head. "She isn't looking for a donation. She needs legal advice." I huffed out a lungful of air. "She's a potential new client."

"*What?*"

"Scott Hutchings removed his wife from their home and is filing for divorce. She's living in a room in Mississauga and needs representation." I paused. "My representation."

"Why didn't she tell me that? She kept insisting on only talking to you, and she refused to tell me why. I assumed it was personal, and I didn't think you would want to talk to her, given your feelings for her husband."

"Soon-to-be ex. You should have put her through, or at least told me and given me the option."

"You're slammed, Halton. You're burning the candle at both ends, and your exhaustion is catching up with you. I was trying to keep her out of your hair. If she had said what it was about, I would have done so, but she refused. I had no idea—I haven't heard anything about their marriage failing."

I found that interesting. Rene heard all the gossip. If he hadn't heard anything, Hutchings had to be keeping this quiet.

I mulled over his words. "From what she said, this hit her out of the blue. I don't know the whole story yet, but she is lost. Her world got pulled away, and she is having trouble coping—not thinking clearly." I had seen it many times with other clients. "I think I believe her, but I need to be sure. I need your gossip connections."

Rene frowned. "I'll make a few calls."

"Good. I need it fast. She's coming in today."

"When did you meet her?"

I told him the story of the bar and her following me. He listened with interest.

"Tenacious," he murmured.

"Desperate too," I replied. "If she's telling the truth, Hutchings handled this all wrong. He, of all people, should know to take the proper steps to end your marriage. You don't kick someone out of their home and abandon them financially. He's creating huge problems for himself."

"Problems you are only too happy to make worse." Rene smirked.

"I'm looking forward to nailing that bastard to the wall."

Rene opened his tablet, scanning the screen. "You're booked solid this morning, and you're in court this afternoon. When do you plan to fit her in?"

"Get me some info, and if her story pans out, call her and tell her to come in at the end of the day. I should be back by six. I'll meet her then, get her story, and figure out the next step. I'll forward you her number."

He stood. "I apologize, Halton. I should have said something to you."

I waved his words away. "Let's see what you find out."

Rene was back in less than twenty minutes. "She's telling the truth. It's hush-hush, but he's been having an affair. Someone overheard them in his office having an argument. His lover laid down the law. Her or his wife. I guess we know which one he chose. Apparently, there is some grumbling between partners as well. Things are not going smoothly business-wise."

I stroked my beard, not surprised to hear she was telling the truth. She would have to be a great actress to appear as desperate and anxious as she had been while talking to me. The news about the office was intriguing too.

"It might also explain his sloppy handling of this situation. He's reacting, not planning. Are you sure your, ah...contact, is telling the truth?"

He pursed his lips and shook his head. "Halton, there is an entire world behind the scenes you know nothing about. Attorneys hang out with attorneys, comparing cases, bragging about their wins, and complaining about their staff. Their staff have their own little community where they complain about all the work they do without recognition for the attorneys and what jackasses most of them are. Of course I'm certain."

My eyebrows shot up. "You tell people I'm a jackass?"

He smirked. "Of course not. I tell them you're the youngest curmudgeon I ever met."

"I'm not a curmudgeon."

"You can either be a curmudgeon or a jackass."

"You're fired."

"Nope."

"Fine. Get me a coffee to apologize."

He chuckled and I grinned. It was how we worked.

"All right. Call Fiona and set her up an appointment for tonight."

"I'll call her right away."

"Maybe get some sandwiches in for us. I'll be busy all day, so I'll need something to eat." Thinking about how slender Fiona was, I thought maybe she would require the food as well. "And a carafe of coffee."

"You want me to stay?"

I paused, then shook my head. "No. I'll talk to her and get the notes. We can meet tomorrow, and I'll tell you what I need. I think she's—" I searched for the right word "—embarrassed and overwhelmed. The fewer people she has to talk to, the better."

"Okay. In here or the library?"

I had combined my law library and boardroom into one large chamber. One end held a conference table for meetings, and the other housed the floor-to-ceiling shelves that contained all the reference books I used. I still had many legal tomes, but I mostly used the internet to cite cases. The law books had belonged to a lawyer I considered my mentor and friend. I kept them in his memory—plus, they looked good in the space, very attorney-ish. There was even a ladder on wheels to reach the top shelves. The library was dark wood with thick carpeting, complete with two deep, comfortable chairs with wide arms I could set my laptop on while searching for whatever facts or cases I was looking for. I used the room a lot.

"Library." I had a feeling she would be more at ease in the welcoming atmosphere of that room. It would keep her calm and focused.

He stood. "On it, boss." He drew in a deep breath. "I am very sorry. I shouldn't have assumed. I heard the name and decided not to add that annoyance to your busy life right now."

I met his serious gaze. "I know, Rene. You were right to be cautious. Let's move forward. Next time, let me decide on that, all right?"

He nodded. "Done."

I walked into the office, silently cursing. Court had run long, and although this time I was successful and my client was happy, it had been a trying day. Today, it was an abused wife fighting for her freedom and trying to start her life fresh with her child. The ex was a brash, arrogant ass who decided that neither of them was worth his time or deserving of his money. The judgment today changed that. We insisted on a lump sum. Once I had the monies for her, she planned to disappear and live somewhere he would never find her. I intended to help her achieve that goal. She was young, still sweet and kind, and I hoped she would find a better life elsewhere.

But now, Fiona Hutchings was sitting in my library waiting for me, and I was over an hour late. Rene glanced up as I strode in. I indicated the library door.

"She in there?"

He stood, straightening his vest. "She is. I explained you were running behind schedule, and she was fine. She said she had her tablet with her and could read until you showed up. I gave her coffee, and we had a chat."

I lifted one eyebrow. "A chat?"

He nodded. "I apologized to her for my assumptions, and we talked awhile. She is quite lovely." He shook his head, pulling his jacket over his shoulders. "She is intelligent. Very gracious." He pondered his next words. "Not what I would have expected from someone married to Scott Hutchings."

I tilted my head, remaining silent, but we shared a look of understanding. Rene had great instincts. If he trusted someone, then it carried a lot of weight with me.

"Your sandwiches and coffee are in there on the table. Your favorite notebook and pens are on your desk. I started a file in the system and a paper one, which is waiting. Do you need anything else?"

"No, go home. I have my laptop and recorder if I need it."

"I assumed you did. Call me if you need anything. I'll lock up behind me."

"Thanks, Rene."

In my office, I dropped my coat, gathered my supplies and

headed to the other room through the door that connected my office to the library. It opened silently, giving me a moment to study Fiona Hutchings.

She was curled up in one of the deep armchairs, looking small on the expansive cushion. The lamp behind her shone brightly against the dark wood of the walls. Her hair was loose again, the intriguing colors vivid under the light. Her head was down, and she appeared to be engrossed in her book. Except I noticed it hung loosely from her fingers and her hand was slack. I couldn't hold back my amusement, and a small chuckle escaped my mouth.

She was asleep.

I sat down across from her, being careful to move quietly. Sleep was precious, and I envied her ability to nap. I wished I could do the same thing. My body felt like cement and my thought process slower than normal. I needed some quality time spent being unconscious. I knew I was going to have to give in and take a pill and hope it helped. I disliked the side effects, but it was time.

I watched her for a moment. Long lashes rested on her cheeks, and her mouth was open, her full lips pursed in sleep. Her sweater hung off her frame, and I could see the weariness on her face. She made an odd clicking noise in her throat as she slept—the sound a steady beat to her breathing. It was somehow endearing. The shadows under her eyes were faint blue—like sky peeking out from under a cloud. Her fingernails were chewed, the skin around the cuticles rough and raw. Even in repose, her hands were clenched. If I had any doubts, they dissipated as I studied her. She was in emotional turmoil. I felt an odd stirring within my chest. I wanted to take away her pain and ease her stress.

I shook my head. What an odd thought.

I was going to be her lawyer. It was my job to do right by her—and I planned on doing exactly that. I was simply worried about my client's well-being, as any good lawyer would be.

I cleared my throat and spoke her name.

"Fiona."

She roused, her head snapping up. She met my gaze, her eyes wide and startled. They were the most brilliant green I had ever seen.

I held up my hands. "Sorry. I didn't mean to startle you."

Her cheeks flooded with color, and she scrambled to stand. "I am so sorry. I must have drifted off. I haven't been sleeping well and the chair was comfortable and the office quiet... Oh God, I'm so embarrassed. Please forgive my behavior, Mr. Smithers."

I frowned. She was apologizing too much for having a little nap. "Not a problem, Fiona. I'm glad you were comfortable enough to relax." I leaned forward, dropping my voice. "These chairs are great for naps. I've had a couple in them as well." I refrained from saying sometimes it was the only sleep I managed to get. Instead, I winked, easing the tension in the air. "As your attorney, your secret is safe with me." I sat back, crossing my legs. "And I told you, it's Hal."

She sank back into her seat, a long sigh escaping her lips. "Thank you, Hal. Your office is nice. I felt quite...safe here."

Her words bothered me.

"You don't feel safe, Fiona?"

Her gaze skittered away. "I've been rather anxious."

"Understandable." Sensing that was all I was going to get out of her at the moment, I indicated the platter of food on the table across from us. "Why don't we eat, and then we can discuss your case?"

"Okay."

I smiled, hoping to put her at ease. "Great. I'm starving."

Fiona

Watching Hal eat fascinated me. He was like a starving wolf, barely sitting down before grabbing a sandwich and tearing into it. He had been the same when I watched him at the bar on Friday, eating his burger with gusto, licking his fingers and polishing off everything on his plate, the look of enjoyment evident on his face.

Wordlessly, I poured him a coffee and lifted the cream, arching my eyebrow in question. He nodded around a mouthful, and I poured in the cream, stopping when the coffee reached a deep caramel color. He accepted the cup, still chewing, and already on his second sandwich. He pushed the plate in my direction, and I took one, nibbling on it, my appetite nonexistent these days.

Scott would have been overjoyed to hear that. He was constantly at me about food. What I should eat or not eat. How much I had on my plate. Constant jabs about how I had let myself go and how amazing his partners' wives looked all the time. It didn't matter what I prepared; he criticized my choice. Criticized me. Dining with him had become akin to having a tooth pulled—it was a painful process. His diet was as rigid as he was, and I couldn't imagine him enjoying something as simple as a sandwich the way Hal was doing right now. Everything Scott ate was done with a disdainful expression, as if the food had offended him in some way.

It probably had.

Hal leaned back in his chair, still eating, although his pace had slowed. He didn't push or ask any questions, allowing me the space I needed. He seemed to be lost to his thoughts, giving me the chance to study him again.

He was a good-looking man. His dark brown hair was swept high off his forehead in a widow's peak, short on the sides, and brushed until it gleamed. He had a moustache and short beard, carefully trimmed and neat. It emphasized the sharp angles of his jaw and full mouth. His eyes were a deep navy—so dark, at first, I had thought them brown, but up close, I could see the blue catching the light. His expression was serious, intense at all times, with shadows that seemed permanently etched under his eyes adding to the severity of his expression. Even when he smiled, he never seemed to relax. Yet, unlike my soon-to-be ex-husband, Hal's intensity wasn't underwritten with a general contempt for everything around him. There was kindness in his eyes—something I had been missing desperately.

Hal was taller than me by at least a foot. He had wide shoulders that tapered to a slender waist and long legs—he wore suits well. I had no doubt they were custom made, the way his jackets clung to those broad shoulders. And he had beautiful hands. Long, elegant fingers with well-trimmed nails. He used them for emphasis when speaking, and I found the actions mesmerizing.

I shook my head at my unusual thoughts. He was my lawyer. Or at least, I hoped he would be. Scott hated him. Despised him on every level. Why, I never understood. He battled with other attorneys and remained impassive, yet Hal seemed to get under his skin. When Scott threw me out, once I recovered from the shock, I knew there was only one attorney for me.

Hal hadn't believed me at first, but something had changed his mind. Whatever it was, I was grateful. I needed his expertise and dislike of Scott to make sure I wasn't railroaded by my soon-to-be ex-husband.

I glanced up to find Hal's gaze focused on me as he sipped his coffee. His plate was empty. In fact, the tray of sandwiches was gone, aside from the mostly uneaten one on my plate.

"Sorry," I mumbled, pushing away my plate.

"You were lost in thought. I didn't want to disturb."

His words made me laugh quietly. "Scott would tell you I often am. He called me a pathetic dreamer more than once."

"Scott is a narcissistic asshole. His opinions matter little to me, and they should to you as well." He arched his eyebrow. "Especially now."

I lifted one shoulder.

"Is that all you're going to eat? I could order something else for you."

"No, I'm fine. Just not overly hungry."

He tapped his fingers on the table. "Forgive me for being blunt, Fiona, but you are much too thin. If I take your case, you need to know it's going to be rough. I've been up against your husband many times, and he doesn't fight fair. It'll be especially bad since he is fighting for himself. I need you healthy and strong so you can fight back."

My bark of laughter was harsh and so was my voice when I spoke.

"Scott would tell you I'm not thin enough." I stood and paced around the room, suddenly too tense to sit any longer. "I was never enough in any way. Not pretty enough. Not smart enough. Not thin enough. Strong enough. I was simply never enough for him!"

Hal didn't react to my tirade, but he leaned forward, resting his elbows on the table. "That right there is what I need. Your anger. I want all the details I require to break him."

"You hate him as much as he hates you. Why?" I asked, curious.

"Because we're opposites. I fight for my client. For what is right. I take on cases I believe in and help people. Scott only wants to win. It doesn't matter to him who he represents as long as the dollars are there. He has no issue using whatever tactic he can come up with—no matter how dirty or underhanded it is—if it means he can win. He wants the notoriety, attention, and money."

I studied him for a moment. "You have all that as well. You have a reputation as a shark in family law."

"One difference, Fiona. I want what is best for my client. I'm an asshole *for* them—not to them."

It was a good analogy. I nodded, frowning, feeling tense and anxious.

He leaned back with a smirk. "Just don't ask my ex-girlfriends their opinion of me." He met my eyes and winked. I had to laugh, knowing he was trying to break the tension. His personal life wasn't any of my concern, although I had heard rumors.

I had to ask the question. "Am I your client?"

He paused before responding. "I have one rule. Truth. You tell me what I need to know—you give me the facts—and I will take your case and do everything I can to win. You lie to me, you omit details because they embarrass you or you hope I don't find out, and we're done. Because I will find them. If you can promise me you can be honest, then yes, I'm willing to take you on as a client."

I sat down. "I'll be honest."

He picked up his pen. "Then let's get started."

FIVE

Halton

"Where do you want me to start?" Fiona asked.

I pulled my notepad closer. "At the beginning. I don't want to hear every detail of your courtship, but I need your history."

She nodded, rubbing her arms as she looked around the room. "We met when I was nineteen. He was older and in law school. He had started late, so there was a six-year difference between us, not that it ever bothered me. I was going for my English Lit degree. I wanted to teach." She frowned ruefully. "I never finished."

"Why?"

"Scott was like a whirlwind. A tornado, really. He swept in and overtook everything. My dad had died not long before I met him, and I wasn't myself. I was struggling. Scott sort of stepped in and filled that void." She sighed and ran a hand over her eyes. "He liked to make decisions, and I was so lost at times, I let him. A year after we met, we were married. I stopped going to school and got a job. The deal was I would work until he became an established lawyer, and then I would go back to school and get my degree, and he would support me."

"That never happened, I assume?"

"No. In between my two jobs, I helped Scott. I was great at research, and he liked it when I worked with him. He said I made him better." There was a sad tone to her voice. "That was back when he was Scott—a young guy with dreams for the future—dreams I was part of."

"What happened?"

She shrugged. "Life, I guess. He graduated and was hired at a firm. He insisted that I still help him. He promised that once he was

37

established, I could go back to school, but that he needed me. He said I knew him better than anyone, and there was no one he trusted more."

"Was it a paid position?"

"Yes and no. He told me, for tax reasons, it was best to let him handle things. He put money in an account for me. He said he was on the bottom rung so there was no money for an assistant for him, and he didn't want to use the pool of assistants they had." She lifted one shoulder. "I know it sounds crazy, but I believed him. I did it because he asked. I was young, and Scott was my whole life. He needed me, and I needed to be needed." She shifted restlessly. "It was my identity—I was Scott's wife. What he needed was more important than what I needed. He kept promising my dreams would happen soon." She smiled ruefully. "Soon never came."

I nodded as I jotted a few notes. I had heard that from other clients. Promises made and never followed through on. Vows that were broken. White lies than became deeper and more complex until trust was severed and lost.

"I was totally under his thumb and too stupid to realize it." She got up and moved around before she spoke again. "Things were okay for a while. He started making a name for himself and was doing well. But he began to change. He became jaded and angry. He yelled more and started picking at everything I did. He decided I only had to go into the office on occasion. He refused to even listen to me talk about going back to school or finishing my degree. He would say, when the time was right, we would discuss it." She smiled ruefully. "The time was never right, of course. He started coming home later, talking less, pulling away more, controlling more and more of what I did, or said—even thought. His opinions became my opinions. I lost myself." Her fingers picked at the sleeve of her blouse in a nervous, jerky motion. "Then one day, he dropped a bombshell. He said he was leaving the firm and going into practice with another couple of lawyers. He said it was the right time and the firm was holding him back. That he wasn't happy."

She fell silent, and I waited. So far, it was the typical story—nothing I hadn't heard before now.

"Scott changed even more once he had his own firm. I didn't like the people he partnered with. They were harsh and vindictive. He started acting like them. He grew cold. All that mattered to him was his career. His image. The firm. I fell to a very distant second—maybe lower. He grew even more controlling and belligerent. I was no longer welcome to help him—I wasn't a *proper* assistant. He hired someone else. A long list of someone elses."

"Was he cheating on you?"

"Yes. I was never able to prove it before, but he told me he was having an affair and no longer wanted to be married." She lifted a shoulder. "He said we could move forward fast with a divorce since he knew I wouldn't forgive him for cheating."

"He's right. It's one of the few ways to speed up a divorce in Ontario and not have to wait a year of being separated. Unless you choose to forgive him and try again." I let that sink in, then asked. "Do you, Fiona? Do you forgive him?"

"No."

She sat down and met my gaze, hers tormented. "He isolated me, Hal. I lost myself. He controlled every aspect of my life. Where I went, who I saw, what I did. School was off the table. We had no children and no chance of ever having them together." She paused, her voice breaking with emotion.

"Was that your choice?" I asked.

"No," she said shortly, and I decided to leave that subject for another time.

"All right. Keep going," I encouraged.

"The house, the business, everything we owned was in his name. I got an allowance, a cell phone, and a car. I was told to be grateful for what I had. He trotted me out to the occasional dinner, then ignored me again." She focused her gaze on the wooden table, tracing the grain of the wood. "We haven't been together as a couple in over four years."

"Why did you stay?"

She was quiet for a moment. "I think for the longest time, I hoped. Hoped he would remember when he couldn't wait to get home to me. That he would find that spark I had seen in him when we first met. I kept thinking it would get better. I did everything I could. I stayed busy volunteering, doing charity work with other wives at the firm since school was no longer an option. I helped out at dinners and functions until Scott informed me he had no desire to attend them anymore. I kept the house immaculate and tried to be a good wife. Anything he asked of me, I did, but it never seemed to be enough. The time just...slipped away while I waited for him. I lost so many years." She blew out a long breath. "My identity was so wrapped up in his, it was as if I no longer existed without him."

I nodded, remaining silent. Once again, her story was familiar.

"From the outside, I had everything. A big house, a successful husband. I drove a new car, I had nice clothes, no money worries. But my life was empty. I was empty. And for the longest time, too weak to do anything about it."

I could sense her growing emotion, so I changed the direction of our conversation.

"Okay. Let's move forward to now. What happened?"

"He came home one night two weeks ago. He told me he was done. He didn't love me and he wanted out of our marriage and there was someone else." She tilted her head. "It didn't shock me, to be honest. He wasn't happy about anything that had to do with me anymore. I had stopped trying as well. I was, ah, embarrassed, if I'm being honest."

I paused in my notes. "Embarrassed?"

"I didn't like the person he had become. Nasty, vindictive, underhanded." Her voice dropped as if confessing a great sin. "I couldn't stand for him to touch me anymore."

"Did you know about his law firm? The kinds of cases he worked on?"

"He never talked about it, but I read the paper. I saw the kinds of people he represented." She shook her head. "He wasn't the Scott I had married. The truth is he stopped being that man years ago."

"But you stayed."

"I had nowhere to go. No money, no job, no experience. All my friends had drifted away from me except for Joanne. She kept in touch, but usually when Scott wasn't around. I'm not sure who despised the other more."

"Is that where you're staying?"

"Yes."

"So he told you the marriage was over. What, then?"

"He told me he owned the house and I had to leave. He handed me an envelope with a bank card and a new account with twenty thousand dollars in it. He said to get a lawyer and he would be sure I was 'looked after.'"

"Looked after? What does that mean exactly?"

"He said I wasn't entitled to much since I never worked or brought anything to the marriage, but he would give me enough to live on until I could find someone else to sponge off." Her hands curled into fists on her legs. "He even had the audacity to say he'd recommend someone to me."

I barked out a laugh. "I bet he would."

"Years ago, he made me sign something that said I would never go after his company."

I rubbed my eyes. "I can always dispute the document. Say it was signed under duress."

"He also told me things have been tight lately and profits are down, but we would work something out." She shifted in her chair. "Then he made me pack a bag, and he drove me to a hotel. He said it was paid for a week, and after that, I was on my own. I called Joanne, and she came and got me right away."

I snorted and set down the notepad. "Okay, I am going to give it to you straight. First off, he is full of shit. You are entitled to your share of the marital wealth. You did bring something to the table. You helped put him through school, and you basically worked for free for years. As for profits, he's trying to scam you, Fiona. He's going to downplay everything to make sure you get as little as possible. His offer to send you to a lawyer would be some underhanded buddy of his who would help Scott screw you over." I ran a hand over my face. "He is such a piece of trash. I'm going to enjoy going after him. I'll drain him of everything. He'll be lucky to have a firm when I'm done."

"This isn't about the money, Hal."

"What is it about, then, Fiona? Tell me what you want."

She shook her head, sadness filling her eyes. "He took away ten years of my life. He made me promises and broke them. Every single one. I didn't get to go to school. I didn't get to have children. I didn't get a husband who would love me and support me for the rest of my life. He stole my independence, my spirit, and my trust. And the worst part is, I let him." She met my gaze, tears swimming in her eyes, her fingers clenching and unclenching on her lap. "He made me into *nothing*. He stole my happily ever after, Hal. He owes me for all that."

An odd feeling rippled through my chest at her words. The sight of her tears did something to me—something I'd never experienced before. The need to be the one to fix this for her was vital.

It had to be me. I had to do this for her. I leaned forward, my hand lifting, the urge to wipe away her tears strong. Surprised at my reaction, I stopped and instead held out a box of tissues. But observing her distress and the way her fists clenched and unclenched on her lap when she was done, I could no longer hold back.

I covered her restless hands with mine. They were cold and shaking. I wrapped them into my grasp and squeezed, wanting, at the very least, to offer her support.

"You, Fiona, are *not* nothing. And for what he stole? He will pay. I promise you that."

Her voice shook as she tried to control her emotions.

"How?"

I rubbed her hands, trying to warm them. To give her a small measure of comfort.

"Leave it to me. If you trust me, I can make sure he pays. But you have to follow my lead. Allow me to do what I have to do. Be prepared to fight." I paused. "It could get ugly when he realizes the one thing he banked on—you simply rolling over and accepting this, accepting everything he says as the truth and taking the scraps he was willing to offer—isn't going to happen. When he finds out who your lawyer is, all bets are off. Are you prepared for that?"

She let out a long, shuddering sigh. Her eyes were fixed on our clasped hands, and I let her think. I knew she was scared and nervous, but if she wasn't willing to face what might happen, we were doomed.

"Don't believe him, Fiona. You are strong. He's hoping you won't fight. But you came to me. You braved my anger to get what you wanted. That alone proves how strong you are. Show him how wrong he was. Fight him back."

She lifted her eyes, determination shining through.

"Yes, Hal, we fight. Whatever you need."

"Good, Fiona, that's good."

"Fee."

I frowned. "I'm not asking you for a retainer. We can discuss all the expenses and come to an understanding we're both comfortable with. I don't gouge my clients."

She giggled, the sound unexpected in the office.

"You find that funny?"

"No," she said, biting her lip to stop laughing again. "I wasn't talking about paying *your* fee. My parents, my friends, they always called me *Fee*. I liked it better than Fiona. Scott thought it was silly and called me Fiona. I want to go back to the name I liked. I want to go back to being the person I liked."

I joined in her laughter at my misunderstanding and nodded in agreement at her decision. It was a small step to reclaiming her independence again.

"Fee, it is."

Fee sat in the armchair again as I made lists of what I needed. Documents I had to have, copies of bank statements, taxes—hundreds of pieces of information I would need to make a case.

"How will I get them?" she asked when I sat with her again.

"I can subpoena them. I'd like to get a look at the bank statements, though. You say he cut off all access to your old bank account?"

"Yes." She paused. "But I had online banking, and the password still works. I don't think he realized I had that access. And I have a spare key. He doesn't know I have it—I had a duplicate made once when I accidentally locked myself out and he had to come home early to let me in. He lectured me about being so careless and interrupting his day. I kept it on a different keychain in my purse after that so it wouldn't happen again. I know he keeps files in his office at the house."

"Okay, I need you to sign in to the bank account and get as many statements as you can. That can start the ball rolling." I paused. "There must be things in the house you want—personal things?"

"A few. It never really felt like home. Scott picked it out and bought it without asking me. He even had it decorated. I never liked it. There are a few boxes in the basement of my parents' things and some sentimental items I would like back. He told me he would allow me to go back one time and pick up anything I wanted to take with me—supervised, of course—and at his convenience."

I snorted. "Fuck his convenience. It'll be at a date of our choosing. Maybe we can snag some of the other records we need then." I rubbed my chin. "I'll get a glimpse of his schedule and demand a date when I know he's in court. Whoever he sends to babysit might be easily distracted."

"How will you do that? See his schedule?"

I cocked an eyebrow at her, earning a small grin.

"Oh," she said. "Don't ask?"

"You got it."

"Okay."

"All right. I'm going to give you a list of things I need you to try to get for me. I want you to write out everything we talked about tonight. Especially his behavior over the past year. As much detail as you can give me." I smiled kindly at her. "Sometimes it's easier to write rather than talk. I'll write out the list, and while I'm doing that can you sign in and get those statements? We can print them out, and I can look them over tonight. No email or texts until we get you a different phone. Scott might be monitoring the one you have, and I want the fact that I have taken your case to come out of left field."

"All right."

She looked pale, and I hastened to assure her.

"I know you didn't think of that scenario, but I know how devious he is. I've got your back, Fee. You can rely on me. Rene as well. We work as a team, and we'll get you through this."

"Okay," she replied, sounding anxious again.

I stood. "Come on, let's get this done, then I'll drive you back to your friend's place."

Unspeaking, she followed me to the computer.

"Use this one—it will print out by my desk. I'll be right there, okay?"

"Yes."

For some reason, I wanted her to relax, to know she wasn't alone.

I laid my hand on her shoulder, feeling her tension. "I got you, Fee. You don't have to face this alone, all right?"

Her smile was tremulous but there. She lifted her hand, squeezing my fingers. "All right." She turned to the computer and started typing.

I hesitated, then walked to my desk, fighting the strangest feeling.

Why did I want to hug her? I didn't hug people. I never got personal with clients.

I glanced back toward Fee.

Why did I have a feeling she might be the exception to that rule?

SIX

Halton

The next day was a shitshow of epic proportions. I was late in the morning due to an accident on Dundas Street. I got a ticket for speeding trying to make up the time. My attitude was shittier than normal when I arrived, and I wound up in an argument with a judge who threatened contempt. I had to step back before I got my ass thrown in jail. Court ran over, I somehow lost my phone, and by the time I headed back to the office, I knew there would be a room full of people waiting for me. It was back to back all afternoon, and I was sure Rene would be going crazy not being able to get hold of me to check what was going on.

I burst into the office, one glance confirming my fears. It was so full, people were standing. I held up my hands.

"Sorry, folks. Bad day at the courthouse. Give me ten minutes to catch up, and we'll get going."

Rene followed me into my office. "Stopped taking my calls now, Halton?"

"Lost my damn phone. I think it might be in the courthouse somewhere. Call and see if it was turned in, okay?"

He set a pile of folders on the desk and added a stack of messages. "You have a long afternoon ahead of you. Did you eat?"

"A stale bagel at the courthouse."

"I'll get you something. Your first appointment is the Sanders about their adoption the birth mother is trying to stop. They won't mind if you wolf something down. In fact, it wouldn't surprise me if she had something in her bag for you."

I chuckled. The Sanders were good people who had provided a stable, loving home for a brother and sister abandoned by their drug-addicted mother. The children were settled and happy, and now the mother was trying to get them back. She was a repeat offender and a huge risk to relapse, given her history. The Sanders were petitioning to adopt the kids, who wanted nothing more than to stay with them. Today was about how to proceed. Mrs. Sanders usually pulled out some cupcakes or muffins she had made me, and I always ate them. I was hopeful today would be the same.

I grabbed the first folder. "Okay. Show them in, and I'll get started." I looked around. "Shit. I need that reference book I was using last week for the Dirks case. Where is it?"

"I put it away. I'll grab it for you after I let the Sanders in."

"Great."

Luckily, Rene was right, and the two muffins I ate while talking to the Sanders helped curb my appetite. After our meeting, I escorted them out and called in the Dirks. I noticed Fiona sitting in the corner and wondered why she was there. I hadn't expected to see her today. Before I could ask, I heard a yell and crash from the library, and I rushed in to find Rene on the floor, the ladder on top of him, a table knocked over.

I hurried over, pulling off the ladder, pushing away the table, and kneeling beside him. He was struggling to sit up, groaning. Blood gushed from a cut on his forehead.

"Stay still," I ordered.

"I'm fine. I just slipped," he replied. "Give me a minute."

"You're not fine," I snapped, using my tie on his bloodied forehead. "Your head is bleeding, and your arm is at a weird angle."

"What?" he responded, glancing toward his shoulder. "Oh."

Then he passed out.

For a moment, I froze. It was Fiona's quiet voice that brought me around. "I called the ambulance," she said. "They're on their way."

I glanced between Rene and the door to the reception area still filled with clients. The phone was ringing, the sound distracting and annoying. "I can't let him go alone," I said. "What am I supposed to do?"

"I'll handle it."

"What?"

"Let me take care of this place, and you go with him."

"I can't ask you to do that."

"You didn't. I offered."

I hesitated, but I didn't have much choice. I had no idea how badly Rene was injured, and there was no way I was leaving him alone. I couldn't walk out of here and leave my clients alone either. I studied Fee, her gaze open and honest, and made a quick decision to trust her.

Paramedics walked in, and I stood so they could help Rene. I turned to Fiona, talking fast. "My clients—get their schedules, and I'll see them as soon as possible. They'll all be contacted tomorrow. Take the phone off the hook. I'll be going out the other door with Rene." I paused. "Wait here."

I hurried to my office, shut the door, and locked the file room. I knew she was telling the truth about her situation, but I was still cautious, and the thought of a stranger alone in my office—the wife of someone I disliked intensely—didn't sit well.

Even if I believed her to be his victim.

I returned to the room. Rene was on a stretcher, in and out of consciousness.

"I'll be in touch when I can," I instructed her.

She began to walk away. "Please extend my apologies," I added.

She looked over her shoulder. "Done."

When he came to, Rene proved to be as stubborn while injured as he was when healthy. He was mouthy and belligerent after getting X-rayed and checked, arguing with the doctors and nurses alike. I had to wrestle his phone away from him, a surprisingly hard feat considering he had one bad arm. He kept texting someone and refusing to stop.

"The doctors told you to stay still. Jesus, Rene! You have a broken arm and a freaking concussion. *Stay down*, man."

He glared, holding the phone over his head. "This is important."

"Nothing is as important as you right now."

He ignored me, typing something on his phone. Then he grinned and let me take it away. His eyes danced, alive with mischief. "I think there is something *far* more important."

I turned off the phone. "Whatever. It's the morphine talking."

"And what lovely morphine it is," he agreed, finally closing his eyes. "You are gonna miss me for the next few days."

I didn't bother to respond—he was already out. He was right, though. I had no idea how I was going to cope without him—and I knew it would be longer than a few days. A temp would drive me crazy, so I was going to have to figure this out once I got back to the office.

I waited until his son arrived, having driven down from Kingston. I filled him in on what the doctor said, including the fact that Rene had to have surgery later today to repair the broken bone.

"They say he can probably go home tomorrow if they get him in tonight, but he'll need help."

Andy chuckled. "Have they met my dad? He'll say it's the useless arm anyway and he doesn't need any help."

I grinned. "Tell him he can't do up the buttons on his jazzy vests with one hand. That'll shut him up."

Andy's wife, Clara, walked in and kissed my cheek. "Thanks, Halton. We'll take it from here. Dad said you had a ton of cases going on right now. You go handle that. We'll handle him."

"I think I got the easy part of the deal," I joked. Then I became serious. "Let me know what happens and as soon as he is out of surgery." I paused. "The firm will cover any medical expenses. He only gets the best."

Rene spoke up from the bed. "Good God, man, I fell off the ladder because my ass was too lazy to move it. I overreached. You aren't paying for that."

"I am, so zip it." I turned to Andy. "Now he's awake, he's yours."

I leaned over Rene. "For Christ's sake, do what they tell you, old man. I need you back at the office."

He grinned, his eyes still not quite focused. "Not as much as you did before."

Then he was out again.

Before what?

I had no idea what he was talking about, but I headed back to the office to try to sort out the mess that would be waiting. Luckily, I was able to grab a cab and get there quickly.

I walked through the door, shocked to find Fiona at Rene's desk.

"What are you doing here?"

She smiled and stood. "I was about to finish up. I figured you'd be along soon."

"Finish up what?"

"Rearranging your schedule. Everyone has been contacted, and I've forwarded the updated calendar to your phone and laptop."

I frowned in confusion and said the only thing I could think of. "I don't know where my phone is."

She indicated the corner of the desk. "Right there."

I picked it up, surprised. "How?" I asked.

"Rene had the app to find your phone. It was under your seat in your car downstairs. I found your spare set of keys, got it out, and charged it for you. He texted me all the information and answered some questions to help me."

Huh. It must have fallen out of my pocket in the car, and in my rush to get to the courthouse, I hadn't noticed. But her words sank in.

"I said not to use your phone. I don't want that asshole—"

She interrupted me with a wave of her hand. "Calm down, Halton. I know the rules. Rene gave me a new phone today. I came to drop off something for you and he had it ready."

It all became clear. "So, you're the person he was texting."

"Yes—and before you freak out, he didn't give me any passwords to private files. Only his applications and the calendar. I got the information to call everyone from there. I didn't touch anything else."

I heard the truth in her simple statement. There was no hesitance on my part in my response. "I believe you."

"As soon as I had what I needed, I told Rene to stop texting me, and I got to work. I told him I had it covered."

"I see. I'm impressed."

Her lips curled in amusement, a teasing note in her voice. "You're impressed because you didn't think I was capable?"

"No, I'm impressed because Rene never gives up control here in the office. I've hired people to help him, and he sends them away."

She shrugged. "What can I say, Halton? I charmed him."

"Knock it off with the Halton shit, Fee. It's Hal."

"Nope. I like Halton. It suits you."

"Obviously, Rene wasn't so drugged he couldn't drop that tidbit."

"Actually, I think it was because he was so loopy. He kept referring to it as *more*phine." She giggled, the sound light and airy. "He was adorable."

I snorted. "Adorable isn't a word I would use to describe Rene. Cantankerous and bossy, maybe."

"Maybe that's why the two of you get along so well. You're twins," she deadpanned.

I began to laugh. This was a side of her I hadn't seen before. I had caught a glimpse of it at the dinner long ago, but now I could hear her sense of humor loud and clear. It hit me as I watched her that she seemed relaxed, almost happy. It was a different look on her.

I liked it.

She ran a finger down her notepad. "I rescheduled all your meetings. You need to be in at six every morning and you'll have to work late the next couple of nights to fit them all in, but I was sure you'd be fine with that."

I nodded in silence. I was usually in before seven anyway. I would come in earlier to get the day started and catch up for the next while.

"I made sure you were confirmed for your court times. I have someone coming in to fix the ladder. I printed out all the documents you need to sign that came in via email. They're by your door." She tapped her chin. "Oh, and someone named Molly called repeatedly, saying she was sorry about throwing water at you and wanted to talk. She kept blathering away until I finally told her you were much too busy for any more emotional outbursts and to go away. And I got your dinner—it's in the kitchen." She indicated the small area Rene where kept coffee and necessities. "I washed the few cups in the sink too."

I stared at her. Gaped, in fact.

I was at a loss for words. A rare thing for me.

She spoke again. "How is Rene?"

I shook my head to clear it. "He's got a concussion and a messed-up arm. He's having surgery tonight or tomorrow to repair it. He'll be gone for a few weeks." I had no idea what I was going to do without him. I looked at the desk in front of her—neat and tidy. "How did you do all this?"

She shrugged. "It's like riding a bike. I did it all for Scott, and Rene is so organized, I was able to find things easily." She indicated his laptop. "He was still signed in to your calendar, and I was able to go from there after he helped refresh my memory a little. That was the priority—to arrange your schedule. The phone calls and emails were simple."

I studied her for a moment. "Did you really tell Molly to go away?"

"Yes." She rolled her eyes. "I think you need to find better, ah, *dinner companions.*"

I chuckled over her statement. It was something Rene would tell me.

"You got me dinner?"

"Yes, I did."

I made a snap decision. "Could I interest you in a temporary position?"

Her smile was wide. "Yes, you could."

I attacked the Chinese food Fee had waiting for me with gusto. She sat across from me, nibbling on an egg roll.

"You need more than that," I said. "Why aren't you eating a combo plate too? It's awesome."

"I had some wonton soup a while ago. I wanted to get you something healthier, but I couldn't leave the office."

"Create an expense file and add dinner to the bill." When she opened her mouth, I glared at her. "That isn't a request. Any meals you get me, or yourself, while you work here are covered. The same with transportation or anything else. You take an Uber to get here in the morning and to go home at night. No more subway. Understand?"

"Okay."

I opened my desk drawer and tossed a set of keys her way. "These will open the door. The code is 872977 to turn off the alarm." I paused. "Those are for the outer office and library. They don't open my door or the door to the file room."

She regarded me intently. "That's fine, Halton. As long as I can get into the front area, I can do my work." She paused. "I know you prefer no one in your office if you aren't here."

"God, morphine makes Rene gossipy," I grouched.

"I understand. I had no privacy in our house. Scott questioned everything. Looked through the mail, insisted on scrolling through my texts and email, not that there was much of either." She sighed. "So, I get it." That was all she said, but her words rang true.

Drawing in a deep breath, I pulled a key off the ring and handed it to her as a sign of trust. "No, you need the file room key."

"Are you sure?"

"Yes. The kitchen doesn't have a key. I like coffee waiting for me when I get here. And toast. Whole wheat toast with butter."

"Nice try, counselor. Rene warned me."

I threw back my head in laughter. "It was worth a shot."

I finished the dinner she brought me and wiped my mouth. "Thanks for that. I've been running on empty most of the day."

"I figured as much. The sandwich Rene got for you is still in the fridge. You can have it in the morning since there won't be any toast."

I chuckled and shook my head. "Okay. I'll call you an Uber and you head home. I'll go through everything on my desk and meet you here in the morning."

I ordered the car and she stood, pushing a small USB drive toward me.

I picked it up, curious. "What is this?"

"That is me, fighting."

"What?"

She fidgeted, then met my eyes. "I used a payphone this morning and called Scott's office. I pretended to be a client needing a lawyer. I said I had to see him immediately. His assistant told me he was in court all day, but he could see me tomorrow."

"I don't understand why."

She huffed out a sigh. "I was around the corner from the house. It runs along a fenced walk to the park. I slipped in the back by the garage, used my key, and it worked."

"No security system?"

She shook her head. "Scott thinks they're bogus and they listen in on you. He refused to get one."

"Ah, that seems a little..." I wasn't sure how to respond to her statement.

"Paranoid," she finished. "He is about a lot of things."

I held up the drive. "What did you do once you got inside, Fee?"

"I got everything I could get off his laptop. Tax returns, investment statements, emails. There was a file marked SHL and Associates, but it was password protected."

"Okay." This was still a ton of information I wouldn't have to pay to get.

A grin played on her lips. "Scott has a problem remembering things like dates, names, and the like. Including passwords. He writes them all down and puts them in a small hidden compartment in a figurine on his desk. He thinks it's clever."

I felt my own grin start. "But you knew where to find them."

She smirked. I found it sexy. With her hair down, her glasses perched on the end of her nose, and looking proud of herself, she was incredibly pretty.

"I do. I did. I have no idea what the files are, but they're on that drive. Do with them what you want."

I tapped the drive on my desk, feeling proud of her as well, and relieved that the asshole wasn't smart enough to have realized she had a key to the garage door and changed the locks, or that he hadn't gone home to pick up a forgotten item. God only knew what he might have done if he had discovered her downloading files. My stomach clenched simply thinking about it.

"That was incredibly brave of you," I praised her, smiling as color flooded her cheeks at my words. "But don't take any more risks. Let me and my team do that."

"I was careful. No one saw me go in or out." She lifted her shoulders. "It was as if I was invisible. The same way as when I lived there."

I knew all too well the feeling of being invisible. But I wasn't going to share that with her. I didn't share that with anyone.

Ever.

My phone buzzed and I stood, crossed to the front of the desk, and extended my hand.

"No more risks," I repeated, pulling her to her feet. "Your Uber is here and paid for. Go get some rest."

I began to step back, but she shocked me when she threw her arms around my waist and burrowed into my chest, holding tight. I hesitated a moment, then returned her embrace. It should have felt strange holding her—yet it didn't. It felt right.

Somewhere inside of me, I recognized how desperate she was for some positive human contact—that she was simply seeking solace for a moment.

But my body didn't get that message. Instead, all I could think, all I could feel, was how amazing she felt against me. The way her head felt tucked under my chin. How soft her body was pressed to mine. When she lifted up on her toes and pressed a kiss to my cheek, the temptation to turn my face and catch her lips shocked me. I cleared my throat and stepped back.

"Thank you for today. For being brave and for helping me."

She shook her head. "Thank *you*," she whispered.

Then she was gone, leaving me standing alone, confused, unsure, and frankly, turned on.

Fuck.

SEVEN

Fiona

I watched the city go past me, the early-morning light catching car windows and reflecting off the glass of the tall skyscrapers that filled downtown Toronto. I glanced at my new phone, pleased to see it was just past five-thirty. I would probably beat Halton into the office again.

I tried to be there before he arrived in the mornings. Regardless of how I had teased him, I had coffee ready for him each day, and once, as a joke, I gave him toast. He had laughed and wolfed it down, as he did any food that appeared in front of him. I enjoyed watching him eat. For so long, I had watched Scott push food around on his plate, pick at everything I cooked or brought in for him. So seeing the way Halton tore into meals, or something as simple as toast, made me smile.

He also made sure if he was eating, that I was as well. He seemed to genuinely care about my health—about me. Another huge difference between the two men. Scott didn't care about his clients—only the money they added to his bank account. And as I discovered, he didn't care about me at all.

I stepped out of the Uber and hurried into the office building. The difference in how I had been feeling the past few days was amazing. It was as if I had a renewed sense of worth. I had a place to be every day. A new sense of purpose. Halton's practice was busy, and the hours flew by. During the day, I was simply Fiona, not Mrs. Hutchings, not the soon-to-be ex, but me.

At the end of the first week, I knew what I wanted, so I approached Halton, setting a pile of documents on his desk.

"These need to be looked over and signed."

He indicated the chair in front of his desk and picked up the pile. "Sit."

He scanned and signed while talking.

"Finding everything okay?"

"Yes, Rene is very organized."

"How often has he texted?"

I chuckled. "Only on occasion. I think his daughter-in-law is monitoring him since he got released from the hospital."

He smirked. "Clara is great." He met my eyes briefly. "But I think he knows the place is in capable hands. You're doing an amazing job, Fee."

"Thank you." I hesitated and cleared my throat.

"Whatever has you all jittery, spit it out," Halton drawled, scrawling his name on the last document and laying down his pen. "What do you need?"

Halton was the same with everyone. He was intense and driven. Blunt and direct. But there was the underlying sense of kindness I had first sensed in him. He treated his clients with respect and dignity. He stuck to his rules—he believed in the cause he took on, or he didn't accept the case. Honesty was important to him. As was speaking your mind. So, I got right to the point.

"I want to change my name back to my maiden one right away. I don't want to wait for the divorce."

He sat back, resting his hands on his desk, his long fingers loosely entwined. "Tell me why."

"I don't want to be Fiona Hutchings, ex-wife of Scott. I want to be me again."

He raised his eyebrows, silently telling me to continue.

"I feel like Fee again. Productive. But when people ask my name, it brings me back to Scott and the past. I want to move forward."

He nodded. "Okay. We'll get the paperwork done. You can do most of it yourself—it's a fairly simple thing. I can help if you need me to." His eyes crinkled in amusement. "How will I address you now—Ms....?" He let his question trail off.

I returned his smile. "Nelson. But we'll stick with Fee. My dad called me Nelly when I was little. He would make up funny songs and sing about his FeeNelly. It always made me laugh."

"You were close with your father?"

"Yes. My mom died when I was younger, so it was only us." My voice dropped. "He had a massive heart attack and died while I was at school. I never got to say goodbye. I still miss him."

"I was fourteen when my dad died," Halton confided.

"Were you close?" I asked.

A mask came over his face. "Not as close as I wanted to be."

"Were you closer to your mother?"

He stood, his voice cold. "Not even remotely."

"I'm sorry, I obviously touched on something personal," I said, sensing his withdrawal.

His face softened. "It's fine, Fee. I don't like to talk about it."

"I understand."

He handed me the documents. "We'll get your name change started. I'll sit with you on Monday as your lawyer, and we'll discuss your case. I should have most of what I need then." He winked. "Book yourself an appointment."

"You're already booked solid, so we can do it after hours."

"Okay," he agreed. "Get dinner in, and we'll talk."

I headed to the door and turned. "Halton?"

He glanced up. "Yes?"

"I'm sorry. I honestly didn't mean to bring up bad memories."

Something passed through his eyes. Hurt, pain—distant memories that haunted him. I could see it. But he simply shrugged.

"It's fine. Don't worry about it."

But for some reason, I did.

Halton

Rene shifted, wincing slightly as his arm moved. I frowned at him, shaking my head.

"You can barely move, and you think you should come back to work?" I reclined back into my chair. "I don't think that's a good idea."

"I'm bored. Clara is like a mother hen watching over me and fussing. She won't let me do anything," he complained.

"I heard that," Clara called from the kitchen. "Stop complaining, old man, or I won't feed you tonight."

"Whatever," he mumbled.

I grinned at their banter. Rene adored his daughter-in-law, and she felt the same for him. I was glad he was feeling better, but he wasn't ready to come back.

"You had a major fall, Rene. You're still recovering from the concussion. Your doctor says you have to take it easy. Between your head and your arm, what good are you to me? Take the time to recover, then come back. Don't push it."

He studied me intently. "I assume this relaxed attitude has something to do with a silver-haired woman who has taken my place?"

I laughed. "Fee hasn't taken your place, Rene. But she's doing a great job. I like her. The clients like her. In fact, I thought when you were ready to come back, you might want to keep her on to help you.

I think you'd like working with her. There's certainly enough work to keep you both busy."

"Mm-hmm," he replied, narrowing his eyes. "You like her."

"I said I did. She's a great temp. Lousy at choosing a husband, but we all make mistakes. At least I can help her with that."

"Uh-huh."

I glared at him. "What are you insinuating?"

He waved his good hand. "Nothing. I'm simply agreeing with you, Halton."

"I call bullshit."

He met my gaze. "So do I."

"Okay, time to change the subject."

He smirked, and I picked up my coffee in order not to reply.

Because he was right. There was more to Fiona than just a temporary fill-in for Rene. And she was more than a client. In the time I had known her, I discovered I enjoyed her company. Her humor and wit. I found her intelligent and quick. I looked forward to the time we shared at the start and end of every day. I liked her. I really liked her. So much so, I found excuses to spend more time with her.

Fiona slid a coffee and two sandwiches onto my desk and turned to leave.

"What are you doing? I asked, flipping closed the file I was perusing for an upcoming meeting.

"Going to my desk to eat lunch."

"Rene and I eat lunch together whenever I'm in the office." I indicated the chair in front of me. "Join me."

She left, then returned with a sandwich obviously brought from home. She caught me eyeing it and rolled her eyes.

"Something wrong?"

"Nope. Nothing wrong with classic PB & J."

"No doubt Rene's lunches were a little more exotic."

"Actually, he ate the same thing almost every day. Chicken noodle

soup. Sally's—his late wife's—recipe. He makes a batch every weekend. On occasion, he shares."

"He's larger than life."

"That he is."

"He must miss her—his wife."

I smiled as I chewed. "Sally loved clothes and style. She knew how to sew and liked to dabble in design. He liked to encourage her, and she always used him as her guinea pig for her ideas. He loved it—and her—and he has never stopped being 'fashionable' as he calls it, in her honor. I'm used to his eccentricities. I never know what he is going to walk in wearing."

"And you wouldn't change it for the world."

I met her eyes. "No, I wouldn't."

"You're very fond of him."

"He is quite the character," I admitted. "He runs this place and me."

She grinned. "He runs them both well."

I chuckled. "Don't tell him that. His ego is big enough."

She winked. "Your secret is safe with me."

I lifted half of one of my thick ham and cheese sandwiches. "Interested in a trade?"

Fee looked dubious. "Really?"

"Yeah. I'm suddenly craving peanut butter. Give it up."

We traded, and I got a strange sense of satisfaction watching her eat part of my lunch. She needed the protein and calories. I made a big deal of eating her little sandwich, humming and smacking my lips over the cheap peanut butter. It was worth eating, knowing I had, in some small way, cared for her.

She stood when she finished. "Thanks for the break."

"My pleasure."

She stopped in the doorway. "Rene told me you always eat at your desk alone, Halton."

I grinned, unabashed at being caught. "Guilty as charged, but you are much prettier, and I've heard all his stories before."

"You were being sweet."

I snorted. Sweet was a word never used to describe me, but somehow, I liked knowing she thought about me that way.

"Keep that to yourself. I have a reputation to uphold."

A flush stole over her cheeks, and her smile broke through. "I will."

I winked. "Good job."

She left me smiling and determined to repeat our lunch.

It was a conundrum. I wasn't sure I had ever *liked* a woman before now. I wanted to get to know her even more. The conversation we'd had about her last name stuck with me. I was proud of her decision and the reasons behind it. She was stronger than she thought she was—wanting to move forward with her life. Eager to embrace the future. Listening to her talk about her parents—even briefly— brought forth an urge to tell her about my parents, which had shocked me. I never shared my past with anyone. But I wanted to share it with her. And I had no idea how to handle it.

"Anyway," I said, setting down my empty cup and pushing my confusing thoughts aside. "I don't want you to hurry back. Take some more time, then ease back in."

"How is her case coming?"

"I've been waiting to see if he makes the first move, but nothing has happened. It's been almost two weeks since she came to see me, and four since he kicked her out. I'm done waiting. Fee is ready, so I have the documents set to go. He's going to be served on Wednesday. I'll go over everything with her tomorrow. I'm going for half of everything, and I'm fighting to get the business agreement struck down. It was signed under duress." I ran a hand over the back of my neck. "I think her entire marriage the past few years has been duress." I leaned forward, resting my elbows on my knees. "He's gonna fucking lose it when he sees she has hired me. It's going to be interesting, to say the least."

"He thought she'd roll over and take what he offered?"

"Without a doubt. He thought he had broken her and he had her exactly where he wanted. That she'd agree and walk away. The cocky bastard even offered to get her a lawyer. Promised her he would look after her," I scoffed. "Look after himself, he meant."

"I guess he didn't know her as well as he thought."

"No, he didn't. She is way stronger than he gave her credit for. He weakened her, but he didn't break her. And I'll make sure she comes out even stronger."

He picked up his cup with a knowing look. "I have no doubt."

I ignored his hidden meaning.

Fee's hand shook as she signed all the documents I gave her. I sat back, worried. I had taken my time, discussed every outcome with her, made sure she understood all the steps, and determined how to hit him to get the maximum benefit. Letting him drag it out had actually been beneficial for us. I made sure Fee was prepared, but now, I had my doubts. Maybe it was still too overwhelming for her.

"Are you sure you're ready for this, Fee?"

Her gaze flitted around the room—one of her tells when she was nervous or upset. It amazed me how many things I knew about her simply from watching and listening over the past days. It had never happened to me until now.

"Fee?" I prompted.

"It makes me nervous wondering how he'll react..." She swallowed, her voice shaking. "What he'll do."

Something in her voice made the hairs on the back of my neck stand up. "Is there something you haven't told me?" I asked.

She didn't respond.

"Did he hit you, Fee?" I demanded, my hands curling into fists of rage.

"One time," she whispered. "One day, it struck me that this was my life. Scott had come home, already angry when he walked in the door. He got angrier because I hadn't picked up his suit at the cleaners. I forgot—I was busy and I forgot. He berated me, and for the first time, I got angry back. I told him I was tired of being his maid and his whipping boy—that I wanted out of our marriage." She shut her eyes as she relived the memory. "He became enraged and grabbed me, shouting and yelling. He threatened me and told me he would never allow it. He screamed all sorts of obscenities at me and told me to forget that idea. He owned me, and he would be the one to decide if the marriage was over. He shook me so hard, I got dizzy. We were standing on the landing midway up the stairs. When he pushed me away, I fell." She swallowed. "He insisted it was my fault."

"Bullshit."

"He told the paramedics I slipped. They believed him." She lifted a shoulder. "By the time I came home from the hospital, I had heard him tell the story so often, I almost believed him."

"What were your injuries?"

"Cracked ribs, a sprained wrist, and a concussion."

"I want those hospital records." Anger exploded in me, and I smacked the table. "Why didn't you say anything? I told you I needed honesty!"

She drew in a deep breath, not meeting my eyes. "Because it embarrassed me, Halton. I stayed with him. I let him get away with it. He never did it again. In fact, unless we were out, he never touched me again. But from that day onward, I was afraid of him in a way I had never thought I would be."

Her words dissipated my anger. I scrubbed my face then leaned toward her, sliding my fingers under her chin and making her meet my eyes.

"I understand. But no more. You swear it was one time?"

"Yes. The rest of the time, he used words." She swallowed, the action moving her throat against my fingers. "Those left marks no one can see, but I feel them every day."

Her eyes were fathomless, the green so vivid and verdant. I could see her pain and again felt the odd pull to erase it.

"I'm sorry," was all I could offer. "But don't be scared, Fee. He's shown poor judgment, but he isn't a complete idiot. He'll get his own counsel, and they'll handle the case. You won't have to put up with him or his words anymore. Just to be safe, I'll pick you up and take you home for a while, okay?"

Her eyes widened. "You don't have..."

I cut her off by tightening my fingers on her chin. "Yes, I do. Let me, please."

Her shoulders sagged. "Okay."

Realizing I was still holding her chin, I released it and sat back. I picked up the documents and slid them into the envelope.

"Ready?" I asked.

She raised her chin. "Yes."

I winked. "Good, FeeNelly. Good girl."

Her laughter made me grin.

I wasn't smiling when I walked into the office on Saturday morning and found her there.

I hadn't been able to settle Friday evening, and I'd tossed and turned even more than usual all night. Insomnia had me pacing the floor, so I gave up and came in to get some work done while the office was quiet. There had been no word from Scott, but I knew that would change soon. Monday was a holiday, and the following short week was going to be a busy one.

I was wary when I opened the door and found the alarm turned off. I saw Fee's purse by the desk and wondered why she was here. My suspicious nature had me check to make sure my office door was locked, then I shook my head. She had already proven herself to me. She was probably feeling anxious and decided to do some work herself. I opened the library door and stopped.

She was asleep in the chair, silhouetted by the dim light coming in the window. Her coat was draped over her, and beside her on the floor was a suitcase.

What the hell was going on?

I sat across from her, taking in her appearance. Her hair was disheveled and unkempt, her face pale and wan. It was obvious she had been crying. My anxiety grew looking at her fingers that clutched her coat tightly, even in sleep. The nailbeds were bloody and raw. She had been fine when I left yesterday. She had plans for a quiet weekend, knowing she would no doubt have to face the start of Scott's battle against her.

Something was terribly wrong.

I laid my hand on top of hers and spoke her name in a low voice. She jerked away with a gasp, her body jackknifing into an upright position.

"Shh, Fee," I crooned. "It's me."

Before I could say anything else, she launched herself at me with such force, it pushed me back into the chair. Feeling the sobs ripping from her chest, I held her tight, talking to her, trying to calm her down.

"It's okay. You're safe."

"I've got you."

"Fee, love, please calm down. I'm here. I'm right here."

I had no idea where those words came from, but they seemed to reach her. She shuddered, but her sobs diminished and she began to relax. I kept her close, running my hand up and down her back in a soothing motion.

Finally, she lifted her head, her eyes red, swollen, and exhausted. Her hands shook as she scrubbed at her cheeks, and I grabbed some tissues for her. She sighed, the sound long and deep, then spoke.

"I'm sorry."

"No. Whatever happened that did this to you, don't be sorry." When she didn't reply, I cradled her face between my hands, making her look at me. "Go wash your face. I'm going to make us coffee, and you can tell me what happened."

"Scott happened," she whispered.

My hands tightened. "Did he touch you?"

"No."

"Threatened you?"

She didn't respond, and I had my answer. The stupid bastard. Whatever he had done, he was going to regret it. I would see to that.

"Go," I said as gently as I could. "It's going to be fine, Fee. I promise."

She slid from my lap, heading toward the door leading to the main office. I stood.

"No, Fee. Use my private one. Have a shower and give yourself a little time to calm down. I'll wait for you here."

"Your-your private one?"

We both knew what I was offering.

"Yes." I pulled out my keys and unlocked the door between the two rooms. I carried her suitcase into the bathroom and left her.

"Take your time."

I made coffee, then stared blindly at the wall. I didn't understand my reaction to her tears. I'd had lots of clients weep in front of me, and I never felt helpless. I never felt the overwhelming need to fix whatever upset them. To find the person responsible and use my fists until they felt the same hurt. I'd certainly never called a client "love" before. It was a pet name my father used to call my mother back a long time ago when they were happy. When we were a family. Why it slipped from my lips when I was holding Fee, I had no idea.

What the hell was going on with me?

What the hell was Fiona doing to me? And why did the thought of those green eyes filled with tears make my chest ache so hard?

I had no idea, but I knew I had to figure it out.

She sat across from me, dressed in casual clothes, her hair piled on top of her head. She looked younger than thirty, although her exhaustion was evident.

I pushed the coffee toward her. "Drink."

She sipped the coffee, holding the mug with trembling hands.

"When did you see Scott?"

"He showed up at Joanne's last night. I was having a shower, and I heard yelling. I went to see what was going on, and he was there."

"Did he touch you?"

She hesitated.

"I want the truth, Fee. All of it."

"He grabbed my arms. He was livid, and he had been drinking. I could smell it on him. And his eyes—they frightened me. There was something weird about them. He was screaming at me that I was using *you*, of all lawyers." Her gaze flickered to mine before dropping again. "He called you 'that low-life do-gooder' and said you liked to mess with him."

I snorted. "I do like to mess with him, but he's mixing his metaphors. Am I a low-life or a do-gooder?"

She shook her head, still not meeting my gaze. "Neither," she whispered. "You are a champion of those of us in need."

Her words did something to me. Fractured a small part of the wall I kept around myself, splitting it open enough to make me reach out to her. I captured her hand in mine, holding it tight.

"Thank you, Fee."

"It's the truth."

I squeezed her fingers. "What happened?"

"He said a lot of things. That I chose you to get back at him. That I was going to regret my decision. He said if I had listened to him, he would have looked after me. That this could have been done with no acrimony, but instead, I had stabbed him in the back by going to you. He swore I would walk away with nothing and I would be begging for mercy when he was done with me. He said I was worthless and a lousy excuse for a wife." She stopped, but I knew there was more.

I almost laughed at his choice of words. He ended their marriage, made her feel like nothing, and didn't think there would be any acrimony? He was more of an idiot than I thought.

"Truth," I repeated, needing the entire story.

"He said I was a lousy lay, but I was probably screwing you behind his back. He swore he had proof. I think he's going to try to damage your reputation."

I wanted to get up and go find him. Beat the shit out of him until he begged for mercy. But that wouldn't do either Fiona or me any good. I had to stay calm for her. "He's desperate and stupid, Fee. He has no proof of any such thing. I'm not the least bit concerned."

"He warned me it was going to get ugly and he was going to make sure I paid for this embarrassment." She let out a quivering sigh. "By that point, he was screaming and shaking me."

She ran a hand over her head, resting her forehead against her palm. "Joanne came into the room and said she was calling the police.

He shouted and cursed some more, and her neighbor showed up. Scott left after that."

"Of course he did. Bullies always leave when threatened. And make no mistake, he is a bully. A stupid one at that." I shook my head. "He's digging his own grave here. Did the police show up?"

"No, Joanne hadn't called them yet."

"Dammit," I cursed. "I would have liked that on the record. But we have witnesses, so that works too."

"He scared Joanne. I don't know what he said to her, but she was so frightened, she was in tears. She had an abusive boyfriend years ago, and it left her skittish. I knew she was scared that he might come back, so I lied and told her I had another place to go. She didn't believe me at first, but I convinced her. I told her I was leaving in the morning, but I left after she was asleep."

I shook my head in disbelief. Fee was more concerned about her friend than herself.

"So, you left? With nowhere to go?"

"I waited until it was late. I knew Scott was gone—we had heard tires squealing after he left. I think he was driving intoxicated."

"A shame he hadn't hit a wall and taken himself out," I stated wryly.

She offered me a small smile, knowing I had been joking.

Sort of.

"Anyway, I waited until about two and left. I walked a few blocks away to a coffee shop and called an Uber. I came here because I knew he wouldn't think to look for me at my lawyer's office in the middle of the night."

"Why didn't you call me?"

"It was late, Halton. I didn't want to disturb you."

"Disturb or bother me, you mean?"

She shrugged, and I knew I was right. I hated the thought of her out in the middle of the night alone, scared, with nowhere to go.

"Fee, I'm your attorney. You can call me anytime. Especially for something like this. Understand?"

"All right," she said quietly.

I glanced at her suitcase. "Were you planning on staying here all weekend?"

"I hadn't really thought about it. I knew I couldn't stay with Joanne anymore, and I had nowhere else to go."

I frowned. "You can't stay here. Sleeping in a chair, living out of a suitcase."

Alone, I added in my mind.

"I called around when I got here, but with the long weekend, a bunch of conventions in town, and some hockey games, the hotels that were close were all booked. I'll make some more calls in a while and find a place."

She shifted, taking her hand away. I hadn't even realized I was still holding it.

She rubbed her arms, wincing slightly.

"Let me see."

She pulled up her sleeves, and I had to hold myself back from cursing and going to find Scott, regardless of the outcome. Bruises were forming on her upper arms. Dark, angry bruises with the distinctive outline of a hand. Scott's hands. I couldn't risk him finding her again. She needed to be somewhere safe.

She looked away as I took pictures of her arms. That bastard was going to pay for this.

Studying her, I made another snap decision. They seemed to come easy when it involved Fiona.

I retrieved her suitcase. "Get your purse, Fee. You're coming with me."

She followed me to the elevator, nervous. I stood close, letting her know I was right there for her. We were silent as I made sure she got into the car. I stowed her small suitcase in the back seat and pulled out of the garage.

"Where are you taking me?" she asked.

"To my place."

EIGHT

Halton

I opened the door to the guest room, placing Fiona's bag on the floor beside the bed.

"The bathroom is across the hall. I know there are towels and things in there. My housekeeper makes sure it's well stocked."

She looked around, obviously still in shock. Aside from gaping at me in the car when I told her where I was taking her, she hadn't said a word.

She sat on the edge of the bed, holding her purse close to her chest.

"You don't like people in your office. You guard your privacy."

I crossed my arms. "Yes."

"But you brought me to your *home*, Halton. I don't understand why."

I didn't know why either, except the bottom line was I couldn't stand the thought of her sitting alone and scared in a hotel room.

I kneeled in front of her, pulling her purse out of her tightly clenched fingers. I wrapped my hands around hers, noting how cold they were. "Because you need a friend."

"Are we friends?"

"I think so."

Despite the situation, she smiled. "I think so too."

"Then you can stay here for the weekend, and we'll figure it out. No one can get to you here, Fee. I won't allow it."

"I'm worried about Joanne. What if Scott goes back and gets aggressive with her?"

"I'll take care of it. Why don't you have a nap? Or take a bath. Or both. Relax and let me make some calls. I'll order some lunch in a while. Anything you fancy?"

"I, ah, love Swiss Chalet." She chewed her lip. "Scott hated it—he said it was common, and he refused to ever have it."

"I like Swiss Chalet. There's one close that delivers. You get some rest, and I'll come get you when it arrives, all right?"

"All right."

I brushed a kiss to her forehead and stood. "You're safe, okay?"

"Okay."

I stopped at her door. "I'm here if you need me."

Tears filled her eyes, and she nodded.

I pulled the door shut behind me, leaning my head back on the wood.

What the hell was I thinking?

"Tell me what to do," I said into the phone.

"Well, for starters," Rene began. "You need to find her a place to live. She can't live with you. That'll give Scott all the ammo he needs to prove he's right. What were you thinking?"

"I wasn't," I admitted. "I just wanted to get her somewhere safe. Where she wouldn't be alone and scared. My place was the only thing that came to mind."

"Your heart is in the right place, Halton, but your logic is out the window."

"I know."

"If Scott Hutchings got wind of that, he would twist it and use it to his advantage. You know how he works."

My head fell back against the chair. "Fuck."

Rene hummed in agreement.

"She shouldn't be working for you either. That might cause an issue."

"Fuck that," I growled. "She does great work. Why should that be an issue? There's no conflict of interest. Her divorce doesn't bring the firm into the case at all except that I'm representing her. He kicked her out, she needed a job, I needed a fill-in. It has nothing to do with the case."

"He'll twist it."

"Then I'll untwist it. I represented you when that asshole tried to sue you for that stupid fence you put up that he thought impeded his view. Same damn fucking thing."

"Calm down, Halton."

"I am calm. I can't figure this out."

"Figure out what?"

"What the hell is Scott thinking? He knows better. He knows the steps to end a marriage with as little fallout as possible. He's the one fucking this up." I paused. "Something Fee said about his eyes. I know he was drunk, but I'm wondering if there is more than alcohol involved."

Rene grunted. "I have no idea. I'll make a few more calls next week. I'm sure the gossip mill will have been working overtime. News of this will spread fast, and suddenly people who didn't want to say anything will have lots of gossip to share."

I huffed out a chuckle. "Okay."

"You need to find her a place."

"I will. I'm gonna make some calls."

"Have you thought of calling Bentley?"

Bentley Ridge was a huge real estate guy. He owned a ton of

places in Toronto. My office was in one of his buildings. His company built the condo tower where I lived. We were friends and did each other favors from time to time.

"Yeah, I will. I hate bothering him on the weekend, but I'll make the call."

Rene paused before he spoke again. "What's going on with you, Halton? I've never known you to act this way toward a client. You've always been a great attorney, but you've never gotten personal."

I rested my head against the back of the chair.

"I don't know," I said honestly. "There's something different about her, Rene. Something about her that brings out some fucking protective gene I didn't know I had in me. I want to kill Hutchings."

"Are you sleeping with her?"

"No." I stated emphatically. I wasn't stupid and I had rules. No married women, no staff, and certainly not clients. Fiona was all three.

"Is it possible you're developing feelings for her?"

"Don't be ridiculous. That isn't it at all."

"Tread carefully, Halton. This isn't just about you. She's lost and confused and looking for a white knight."

I sighed. "I will, Rene. I only want to help her."

"I hope you remember that."

I hung up and scrubbed my face.

Despite my assurances to him, I hoped I did as well.

I dialed Bentley's number, not surprised when he answered right away.

"Hal. What can I do for you?"

I chuckled. We rarely wasted time with pleasantries. "Bentley, I need a favor."

"Name it."

"I need a place for a client to stay. Short term. But somewhere close to my office and secure."

"How big?"

"Space isn't a priority. Security is."

"Time frame?"

"As soon as possible. And it would be for a couple of months, maybe a little longer. It's a divorce case."

"Anyone I know?" he asked dryly.

"Fiona Hutchings."

There was a pause. "As in, Scott Hutchings? The man you loathe?"

"Yes."

"And you're representing his wife?"

"Soon-to-be-ex, yes."

He whistled, long and low. "Wow. That's going to be interesting. He's going to blow a gasket when he finds out who she hired."

"He already did. That's why I need a place for her to stay."

"Where is she now?"

"Ah, in my guest room."

This time, the silence stretched on. "Hello?" I asked, thinking I'd lost him.

"Let me get this straight, Hal. Your client—the soon-to-be ex-wife of the man you hate—is currently sleeping in your guest room?"

"Well, I think she's having a bath right now. Then we're going to have Swiss Chalet. She likes that."

"You're having Swiss Chalet," he repeated, sounding incredulous. "What the hell are you doing, Hal? You never let anyone in your personal space." He hesitated. "Are you involved with her?"

"No. She's a client in trouble. I'm helping her."

"I've never known you to go to this much effort for a client."

I was tired of having this conversation with people. "Well, there are extenuating circumstances. Can you help?"

"I'll make some calls. Aiden will be in touch this afternoon."

"Thanks, Bent. I owe you."

"All I want is the whole story, Hal. Because no matter what BS you're telling me, there is more to this than a client in trouble."

He hung up.
I stared at the phone.
Was he right?

Fiona

I padded into the living room, more relaxed, but still feeling nervous. I was in Halton's home. His most personal of places. I had learned in the time I had been working for him how private a person he was, so I knew this was a big deal.

I took in the room. It was large, with floor-to-ceiling windows that offered a gorgeous view of the lake from one side, and downtown Toronto from the other end of his corner unit. Tall ceilings, dark hardwood floors, clean lines, and lots of grays, navy, and black made the space comfortable, albeit totally masculine. It was the penthouse and took up the entire floor, which was hardly surprising, given how he liked his privacy. He was the only one with access to this floor, so he never had to worry about neighbors asking for a cup of sugar. He controlled who could be at his door.

Which was the reason I was still confused as to why I was here.

Halton came around the corner, his phone tucked in between his shoulder and ear. He held a bag in his hand, and smiling, he indicated the kitchen with the tilt of his chin. I followed him, unpacking the bag as he grabbed some plates from the cupboard.

"Great, Aiden. I appreciate it. Wednesday will work fine."

He hung up and looked at the containers as he sat at the island. "I'm starving."

"A whole chicken plus all these sides, Halton?"

He grinned and held up a container. "And pie. I love pie."

We opened the containers and Halton dug in. I tried not to stare at him while he ate. It was almost primal the way he tore into his meal, picking up the drumstick and pulling the meat off with his teeth, dragging fries through ketchup and dunking the bun into his Chalet sauce. His manners were evident, but it was obvious how much he enjoyed his food as well.

He stopped mid-bite and swallowed, frowning at my plate. "I didn't get the right things?"

"What? No, it's great."

He shook his head and pulled my plate closer to him. He added some fries, more chicken, and a roll, then pushed the full plate back toward me. "I told you I need you strong. Healthy. A salad with a little chicken on top isn't going to cut it, Fee. Eat up."

I picked up my fork, trying not to roll my eyes as he added even more chicken to my plate and drizzled dressing on the salad. "Better," he mumbled gruffly and went back to eating.

For a few moments, there was only the sound of chewing and utensils scraping across stoneware. Then he spoke.

"I think I have a place for you to stay."

"Oh?"

"My friend's company has a spare unit in the building right behind this one. They share the same parking lot and are connected with a walkway ten floors up, so it's convenient. BAM uses it for interns and the like on occasion. He thinks it's available as of Wednesday. Aiden is going to confirm and will send me pictures shortly. It's a studio, but it works since you can drive to and from the office with me, so you're safe." He met my gaze. "You can't stay here with me, Fee. It would look all sorts of wrong."

I stared at him, aghast. "I didn't expect you to let me stay here,

Halton. Even a few hours is more than I expected. I was going to make some calls this afternoon and find a hotel."

He shook his head. "No. You can stay here until Wednesday. Downtown is booked solid for the weekend, and there is no sense in you getting a room for a couple of nights then moving back to the building. You can stay here until then."

"I don't want to impose."

"You're not imposing." He slid a key and a pass card toward me. "You'll need these until then. The pass card is for the building and the elevator, the key is for the condo."

I accept them silently, feeling overwhelmed at his trust.

He emptied his plate, then took the rest of the chicken and salad and finished off the fries. He held up the last roll. "You want this?"

"Um, no."

He frowned, looking at my plate. "Eat."

Obediently, I picked up my fork, startling when he laid his long fingers over mine. "I'm sorry, Fee. I shouldn't be ordering you to eat. I'm simply worried."

I patted his hand. "It's fine. I'm not used to being able to eat freely. Scott had me so obsessed with not eating, I forget it's okay to want to eat something."

"It *is* okay." He stressed. "Anything you want. Name it and we'll have it. Maybe pizza later when I get back."

He was leaving me alone in his home?

"You're going out?" I confirmed. "I can go wander around while you're gone."

He sighed. "No, Fee. Stay. Nap. Read. Relax. I want you to stay put unless you really want to go somewhere."

"No, an afternoon of reading sounds awesome. Do you, ah, have a date?"

He flicked open the lid on a piece of pecan pie. He met my eyes while chewing and swallowing. "No. Every Saturday, I volunteer my time at a...place. It's a group of dads who are fighting to get custody of their kids. I'm one of a couple of lawyers who donate their time and advice. I take on a few cases for free as well when time permits."

"Halton, that's amazing. Is there anything I can do?"

He finished his pie, closing the lid. "No. Not today, anyway."

"I had no idea you did that. I didn't see anything on your schedule or any pending case files," I mused, thinking of the orderly file room.

"I keep those files in my desk. Rene knows I go there every Saturday, and I don't like it on my schedule. I do it because it's something I believe in strongly, not to look good. Part of the deal is I don't talk about it. I'm just there to help someone get a chance to be with their kids. If I can help fight against the system, then my work is done."

I could sense his hidden emotion. I slid my hand across the island, slipping my fingers through his. He stared down at our hands, but he didn't pull away. "I sense a story, but I understand. I think it's a wonderful thing you do."

He stared into space for a moment. "People automatically assume the child is best left with the mother. It's not always the case, and I help men fight for their rights. If I think their kid is better off with them than the mother, I help. Sometimes, it's advice. Other times they need more. I make sure they get the right attorney, or I take them on—pro bono, usually. At times, all I do is listen as they talk. Sort of like therapy. There are a few other attorneys who do cases like this as well. We keep it on the down low. We're there to help, not for the glory."

I squeezed his hand in understanding. The man across from me was so much more than he gave himself credit for. He disarmed me with his quiet words and conviction. Halton looked up, his navy-blue eyes filled with memories of the past.

"I wish my dad had had someone to fight for him," he said. "Instead I was stuck in a system that believed the lies my mother spouted. That stuck to the belief that the child was best left with their mother—that the father should contribute financially, and have visitation, but not be the governing influence in their life." He barked out a pain-filled laugh. "I often wonder if I'd be as screwed up if they had allowed my dad to raise me."

I frowned, confused. "I don't think you're screwed up, Halton."

He looked down at our hands, still clasped on the cold granite. He lifted them, studying the veins on my wrist, gently tracing the faint blue lines. His touch made me shiver.

"I can't commit to one person," he stated, his voice low and sad. "I don't believe in love or marriage, Fee. I'm the guy people call on when love turns to hate, because it's what I know the best. Hate. I know how to exploit it. Get what I want from people. Pit them against each other and feed the anger. Blow the hell out of the emotions they once embraced and turn them into ash. That's what I do."

I was silent, digesting his words. He kept talking.

"My entire adult life is a string of emotionless encounters. A few attempts at relationships based on sex and not feeling. I've been very upfront with my partners, although a few of them thought they could change how I felt. But I proved them wrong. I don't want the trap of marriage. I don't want kids because I think the world is a messed-up place, and selfishly, I don't want to bring another person into the craziness. I certainly don't want a kid who is like me in any fashion." He sucked in a long breath. "I witnessed the way people use their kids to inflict pain on the person they used to profess to love. I know what it's like to be the pawn in that game. I would never risk it. Ever. I will never allow myself to count on someone else. To trust any one person and allow them the chance to hurt me. I depend on myself. The one thing I care about the most in the world is me. Nobody else."

"I don't believe that. Not for a moment."

His grip tightened. "Why would you say that?"

"Have you listened to yourself? What you do for people? What you've done for me?" I waved my hand. "You've let me into your home. You've trusted me—someone associated with a person you hate. You care about your clients. Your friends. About children. Look at the way you care about Rene. How can you call yourself selfish? Uncaring?"

He pulled his hand away and stood. "I care to a point and nothing more. Rene is a trusted friend who has proven his loyalty—he is an exception."

"What am I?" I challenged him.

He lifted a shoulder. "Another small exception, I suppose. A client who needs more effort than others."

"And once I reach my saturation point, you'll stop caring?"

He sighed, dropping his head to his chest. "I do the best I can do, Fee. I'm not capable of love. It's that simple."

"You are so wrong."

He snapped his head up. "I don't believe in love, Fee. That is a fact. It's an illusion, easily shattered, often abandoned, and rarely real."

"But you admit it can be real? You said you had friends who are married. You must see that love can exist?"

"I suppose there are exceptions. Would you say you believe in love? After what Scott has done—" he lifted his fingers into quotation marks "—in the name of it?"

"I'm smart enough to know what Scott has done has nothing to do with love. I'm hopeful enough to think I might find real love one day. To become *that* person to someone—the one you would move heaven and earth for, do anything to be with."

He smiled, the movement forced. His eyes said so much more than he could ever express.

"Then I hope you find him, Fee. I really do." He passed a hand over his face with a sigh. "I have to go. I'll see you later. Make yourself comfortable."

He turned and left, leaving me sad and confused.

How could he not see the person I did? His self-loathing shocked me. His refusal to see anything but the negative in himself was unsettling. His kindness to people. The care he showed those he loved. Because I believed he did love. He simply refused to see it—or was too frightened to admit to the feelings. Something in his past made him unable to see the good inside him. His horrendous childhood had left him unable to recognize it.

I heard the door close and I stood, clearing away the containers.

Halton Smithers had a lot of love to give. Of that, I had no doubt.

How could I get him to see it?

And why was it so important to me?

NINE

Halton

I glanced through the photos on my phone. "This is great, Aiden. I'll take it. Bill it to the firm, all right?" I planned on adding it all on to Scott's invoice. He kicked her out, so he should be paying for her rented accommodation. I had already explained it to Fee, and she was fine with it as long as I recovered my expenditures. When she had inquired if this was how I would handle it for all my clients, I had to hide my amusement and not tell her she was the only client I had ever gone to this much effort for. I kept that information to myself. I simply assured her it was.

Aiden's voice was filled with concern. "Bent told me who this was for. Are you sure about this, Hal? I mean, the wife of your enemy?"

I was getting bored of the subject. I fucking knew what I was doing. I was a grown-ass man, for God's sake. I rubbed my eyes, suddenly exhausted. It was as if the sleepless nights, Rene's accident, and Fiona's appearance in my life had hit me all at once, and I felt weary. My voice was sharper than usual.

"She's a client, Aiden. Nothing more. I know Scott and his vile temper. He tried to get at her last night, and if he is angry enough, he might try again. It may seem over the top, but the security in the buildings will give her peace of mind. Which gives me peace of mind so I can do my job. Get her a divorce and what she deserves out of that bastard. Nothing more," I repeated.

"Okay. It seems out of the ordinary for you."

I held back my retort and counted to ten. "Send the keys to the office and whatever you need signed, Aiden."

"You'll have them Wednesday afternoon. The place will be clean and ready."

"Thanks. I mean it. I appreciate it."

I hung up before he could ask me anything else. Like where Fee was staying until Wednesday. Rene almost had a fit when I told him. Luckily, I'd had to hang up when I arrived at the community center to donate my time to Dads Seeking Justice.

But I had been distracted all afternoon, having to ask people to repeat themselves, and forgetting to keep my usual meticulous notes.

"Hal!"

I stopped by my car and turned to see Carl, one of the organizers, hurrying toward me. I pushed my door closed and waited for him.

"What's up?" I asked when he got closer.

"I wanted to check on you. You, ah, weren't yourself."

I had hoped nobody noticed. "Sorry. Heavy caseload right now, and I didn't get much sleep last night. I was a little distracted."

He laughed, running a hand over the back of his neck. "That's one word for it. You were glowering at the floor so hard, I thought you'd burn a hole in it. Anything else on your mind?"

"No. Just dealing with another asshole trying to push someone around."

He grimaced. "I hear you. I'm glad they have you on their side, then. Listen, maybe you don't have time, but it's Jay's birthday tomorrow and since you were such a huge part of us getting custody of him, we'd love it if you stopped by for a slice of cake. If you have time," he repeated. "Chase made this huge chocolate cake that looks wonderful. It's casual. Party at one, cake about three."

I had fought to get Chase and Carl custody of Carl's son when he and his wife split up. She didn't want Jay, but she didn't want Carl to have him either. Her homophobic tendencies came out loud and clear during the case, as did her possessive, crazy side, and it ended up costing her custody. Jay was happy and settled with his two dads and I always tried to keep up with my clients and their lives.

"Sure," I agreed. I liked cake, and I'd always liked Jay. He was a cute kid. It would give me something different to do.

Except Fee was at my condo and I didn't want to leave her alone again. I had a feeling Fee liked cake too, and I spoke before overthinking the situation.

"Could I bring a friend? She's having a hard time and could probably use the distraction."

"The more, the merrier."

"Great. See you tomorrow."

I climbed in my car, shaking my head. Why had I asked about bringing Fee?

What was this woman doing to me?

I stared at the steering wheel, reluctant to admit I didn't really want to go home. I didn't know what would happen when I arrived. I had no idea what possessed me to say anything to Fee. To talk about my past or attitude in regard to love, marriage, or children. It was as if the words just spilled out. Her refusal to accept that I was the person I knew myself to be proved to me that she was so damaged by Scott's treatment of her that Rene was correct. She saw me as her white knight, saving her.

I was anything but.

I was a moody, selfish, arrogant man. I lived the way I wanted with no worries about how others saw me. I fought for my clients because it fed some small piece of me that needed to see that justice happened. As if making up for my past by ensuring the kids went to the right place and were looked after. But she was wrong if she thought me capable of love.

I did care for people. Rene, in many ways, was a surrogate father to me. His opinion mattered. He mattered. I cared about the few people I called friends. I cared about my clients.

But love?

That word didn't exist in my world. Not now.

Love hurt. Destroyed you. Made you weak. I had witnessed it too often. Felt the bite of its loss. The sting of allowing my heart to feel more than it should.

I thought about Fee. The things I had learned about her. The softness she had hidden under her mask. The fear and worry. The intelligence and resilience she was rediscovering. She made me laugh. I liked hearing her laugh. I enjoyed our conversations. I enjoyed *her*.

With a sigh, I started the car. I liked her. I could admit that. In any other circumstance, I probably would have pursued her. Had mind-blowing sex with her. And then once that fire had burned out, as it always did, walked away from her.

The saturation point, as she called it.

But it would never happen. For so many reasons aside from the fact that she was a client.

She believed in a world I knew to be false. She wanted that world.

I hoped she'd find it. Because she deserved to be happy.

I shouldn't have brought her into my home. It was foolish and dangerous on my part, but I wasn't going to send her away. It was only until Wednesday. A few nights and days. It meant she was safe, and that was why I did it.

I pulled into traffic, heading back to the condo. I would go and be her attorney. Her friend. Guide her from this point in her life to her next chapter, where she would move on. That was all.

I ignored the small frisson in my chest that felt intense sadness at those thoughts.

I had myself convinced of the ease of the next few days until I walked in the door and the scent of something delicious hit me right away. I followed the aroma to the kitchen, to find Fee stirring a pot and humming softly. She had her hair piled on top of her head, a pair of jeans with a long-sleeved shirt that clung to her torso, and a tea towel tucked into her waist like a quasi-apron. Her feet were bare, tapping out an uneven rhythm on the tile floor. She looked adorable. And sexy.

Dammit.

"Hey," I said, attempting to act casual.

She whirled around. "Hey, counselor. I didn't hear you come in."

A grin tugged at my lips at her nickname. "With all that racket you're making, I'm not surprised."

Her laugh was delightful.

"Sorry, I like to hum when I am cooking."

I winked. "Teasing. What, exactly, are you cooking?"

"Homemade pasta sauce."

I frowned. "How on earth are you making that when the fridge was so empty?"

"Don't get upset," she started, holding up her hand. "There's a Rabba downstairs. I never left the building. I cut through the lobby."

I couldn't really get upset. Her sauce smelled too good and I was hungry. I often ran downstairs to Rabba. They were a local food chain with a great hot-food counter and an amazing selection of groceries and produce. Pricey but handy. I sat down at the island. "Not upset. I'm too hungry to be upset."

She shook her head. "You're in such good shape, but you eat more than I think I've ever seen before. You must burn it off with all that nervous energy."

I chuckled and reached over to the wine rack, selecting a bottle of red. "If you think I eat a lot, wait until you meet Aiden. The man is a walking garbage disposal."

"Charming."

Standing, I grabbed a couple of glasses. "He's a great guy. Bentley's right hand and partner. Maddox is the third one of the team."

She chuckled. "I've heard of BAM. They're a bunch of good-looking guys. They're in the paper a lot."

I wasn't surprised. They were huge players in the Toronto real estate market. But for some reason, it bothered me she mentioned their good looks, and I couldn't let it go.

"I'm in the paper too."

"Yep."

"You said I'm in good shape."

She peered at me over her shoulder. "I did, counselor. You want to cross-examine me? Am I under oath?"

I laughed at her wit. "I've been told I'm a good-looking guy."

She shook her head, her shoulders shaking with mirth. "Now you're fishing."

Unable to resist, I sidled up behind her, resting my hands on her hips. I rested my chin on her shoulder. "Did I catch anything?" I murmured.

"As if I need to tell you how handsome you are."

My lips hovered close to her ear. The delicate shell was pink and glowing. From the heat of the sauce or my closeness, I wasn't sure, yet I wanted to find out. "A guy likes to hear it on occasion."

She shivered. "You are, counselor. You know it."

"Damn right." I pressed my lips to her skin briefly, lightly, the temptation too difficult to ignore. "Don't you forget it."

"With that ego of yours, it's highly unlikely."

I grinned and inhaled deeply. "It smells so good."

"Me or the sauce?" she quipped, but I heard the tremor in her voice. I knew I was riding a dangerous line here, but I couldn't seem to stop myself.

"Both."

"Ha. Nice try. I think I smell like garlic."

She didn't. This close to her neck, I could smell flowers and citrus. Soft. Sweet. And sexier than it should be. But I knew if I said it, there was no going back, and that wasn't fair to either of us.

"Well, no worries about vampires, then."

She laughed and elbowed me out of the way. Regretfully, I stepped back, even though I knew it was the right thing to do. Strangely enough, though, I had liked how she felt molded to my chest. I cleared my throat and got busy opening the wine.

"Did you rest?"

"No, I read a little, made the sauce, and dessert."

"Dessert?"

"A fast trifle. I saw all the berries downstairs and decided that would be great after the spicy pasta sauce. I soaked the fruit in some Amaretto."

"Sounds delicious."

She asked about the group, and I filled her in a little on some of the things I had paid attention to. Before I could change my mind, I asked her about going with me for cake the next day. She seemed pleased and agreed to it. I helped set the island for dinner, feeling strangely content. I had been worried there would be awkwardness between us because of our earlier conversation or that she would want to delve more into it, but she was simply Fee. Sweet and funny, charming, and cooking dinner for me in my kitchen.

Like she belonged there.

I quickly dismissed that thought. I was so tired, my brain was misfiring—that had to be it.

After two huge plates of pasta and salad, I sat back with a groan. "Wow, you can cook."

"I'm a little out of practice. I think the sauce needed more basil."

"It was awesome."

"Dessert now or later?"

"Later. I thought we could watch a movie if you'd like?"

Her face lit up. "I would love that!"

"Great. Go pick something on Netflix. I'll clean up."

"But—"

"Nope. You cooked. I'll clean."

She laid a hand on my arm. "Okay."

She hurried away. I wondered how it was possible that I felt the heat of her touch all the way through my shirt. I shook my head at my stupid thoughts.

It had to be the wine.

The wine kept fucking with my head all night. Add in the exhaustion, and I was practically delirious. It was the only explanation I could come up with for the events of the evening.

Fee chose a suspenseful thriller movie, then kept hiding behind a pillow and gasping in shock at things that seemed so obvious to me. I kept laughing, finding her antics amusing.

Finally, I gave up and patted the seat next to me. "Come here, scaredy-cat."

She scooted over, sitting close.

"You know, we can change channels. Watch something else."

"No," she insisted. "I want to see what happens to the guy."

"In order to do that, you need to stop covering your face," I informed her, draining my wine and leaning back. I lifted my arm and tugged her close. She nestled into my side, her head resting against my shoulder. It felt oddly right for her to be there—the same way it had for her to be in my kitchen. I gave up trying to figure it out and rested my cheek against her hair. I could smell her fragrance again—light and airy. It suited her. Not overpowering but soft.

She jumped, and I rubbed her arm. "It's fine, Fee. It's a movie."

"I know."

The movie ended, and I switched channels to an older film I thought she'd like. I had seen it several times and enjoyed it. No one died, and there was nothing scary—only some bad acting and a thin plot. She relaxed a little, her body leaning closer as she calmed. The death grip she had on the pillow eased, and her hands became still. My fingers found the ends of her hair, and I rubbed the silky strands between my thumb and index finger.

"Your hair is so different. You know, when I saw you in the bar... At first glance, I thought you were a cougar trying to pick me up."

She giggled, the sound feminine and different to my ears.

"I know it's been a long time since that dinner when we met," I mused, "but I'm usually better at remembering people. I should have known it was you."

"It's the hair," she said, tousling the strands with her fingers. "And I don't wear much makeup now. I never liked it."

"Is this, ah, natural?" I asked. "I remember you being blond."

"The blond was fake. This is real. Scott hated it—he said it made me look old and therefore made him look bad. We argued when I let the blond fade and the real colors show through. My mom went white young, and so did I."

"I like it," I murmured. "It's unique—like you."

"Thanks," she said, then sighed. "Don't feel bad about not remembering me, Halton. Back then, it was my job to be forgettable. Scott wanted a presence—the veneer of a happy marriage. I was to look good and smile, but not overshadow him in any way."

A ripple of anger tore through me. I pressed my lips against her crown and squeezed her shoulder.

"You, Fee, are never forgettable. I may not have recognized you instantly, but once I did, all I recalled was how incredible I thought you were, and that you—in every single way, without even trying— overshadowed that asshole. You were simple perfection sitting beside a jerk."

She tilted up her head. Her green eyes glimmered in the low light.

"Thank you, Halton. That is the nicest thing anyone has ever said to me."

I kissed her head again, resting my cheek on it, unable to say anything else.

We watched the movie in silence, and soon, Fee felt heavier beside me. Not long after, she was asleep. Her breathing became deep and even, and soon, she started emitting the strangest sounds I had ever heard. It was a sort of clicking-purr noise. I had heard it in the library, but up close, it was even odder. It reminded me of something, but I couldn't place it. It amused me though, but I stifled my laugh and turned down the volume so she wouldn't be startled awake. I leaned back my head. I would sit here with her for a bit then wake her and go to bed. Maybe my body was tired enough I would get a few hours rest tonight.

It would be a nice change.

Something tickled my nose and I lifted my hand to wipe at it, but it was gone. There was an odd sound close to my face, and my body felt warm and constricted as if I were being held down. I cracked an eye open to figure it out and was shocked to see I was lying down on the sofa.

And tucked beside me, wrapped in my arms, fast asleep, was Fee. I blinked to make sure I wasn't dreaming, but she was there, and this was real. Carefully, so as not to disturb her, I checked my watch. It was almost seven in the morning. I had somehow, by some miracle, slept for over nine hours. I couldn't remember the last time that had happened.

But how? The last thing I remembered was Fee falling asleep next to me. I had shut my eyes, and I must have fallen asleep myself. Somehow, we ended up twisting and turning until we were lying down and had slept the night away. The TV was still playing, the sound low, the table lamp on, and the room dim. I looked down, surprised to see how tightly entwined we were. Our bodies aligned, my leg wrapped around hers, her toes resting on my calf. Our chests were melded together. Her head was tucked into my neck, and I held a fistful of her hair in my hand. My cock was awake too, pressed into her hip, hoping to get closer. I chose to ignore that fact, concentrating on the more important issue at hand.

I had slept with her all night, not waking once. It was the longest I had slept in months, maybe years. I felt rested, rejuvenated. I felt like a million bucks.

Holy fuck.

Fee's eyes flew open, and I realized I had spoken out loud and woken her up. She met my gaze, the vivid green shocked.

"What-what are you doing?"

"Ah—sleeping?"

"Why are you in my bed?"

"I'm not. Neither of us is in a bed. We fell asleep on the sofa."

"Together?" she squeaked. "All night?"

"All night." I stretched, my body feeling the effects of the too-soft sofa. Unfortunately, by doing so, I tugged her closer and she felt exactly how awake I was. All of me.

She scrambled up, pushing away. Her hair was a mess, no doubt from my fingers being buried in it all night. There were creases on her face from my sweater, and she looked panicked. I held out my hands.

"Relax, Fee. Nothing happened. We fell asleep."

She shook her head. "You don't understand."

I pulled myself up into a sitting position. "Understand what? There's nothing to be upset about. It was totally innocent."

Mostly. The cock pressing against the zipper of my pants had another word for it.

"I never sleep through the night," she whispered, meeting my eyes. "Not for years. I'm usually up, pacing a lot—or tossing and turning."

Once again, I had only two words to say.

Holy fuck.

TEN

Halton

After my last expletive, Fee slipped off the sofa and hurried down the hall to the guestroom. A few moments later, I heard the bathroom door shut and the shower come on. I headed the opposite direction to my room and the large en suite, and turned on the shower, letting it warm up before stepping in. The heat felt good on my shoulders. I was stiff from the odd position I had slept in, but my mind was alert and my head clear. The hot water would help ease the stiffness in my muscles.

I ran my hand down my torso, wrapping it around my cock. I bit my lip to hold in my groan as I stroked myself. Images swam through my head, and I stopped fighting them.

Fee laughing. Teasing me. The way she looked this morning with her hair disheveled and her eyes wide. How she felt nestled against me. I leaned on my forearm, my hand moving faster as my imagination went into overdrive. Fee under me, moaning my name. Her lips wrapped around my cock. Her pussy milking me as I thrust into her. I came hard, my release spraying long ropes over the gray tile. My head fell forward, resting on my arm as I caught my breath. I reached for the soap, absently going through the motions as my thoughts careened through my head.

Why had I slept? Because I was so exhausted, my body had finally given in? Or did it have something to do with Fee? Was that possible? I thought of her confession. I had never met someone who had the same problem sleeping as I did. Although, I had to admit, I rarely spoke to anyone about my lack of sleep. Fee suffered from it as well. But together, we had slept. I needed to know more. I had to talk to her.

I shut off the shower, determined, one other question echoing in my head.

Why was Fee so firmly entrenched in all my thoughts?

I narrowed my eyes, studying Fee seated next to me at the island. She had coffee ready when I came into the kitchen and was calmly reading on her tablet. A bagel waited for me, and after mumbling a thank you, I sat down and ate it, sipping at my coffee.

She looked calm, the pale shadows under her eyes decreased. I had been shocked to see the constant look of exhaustion on my face had lessened when I looked in the mirror this morning. One good night's sleep had erased a lot of the deep circles.

I cleared my throat. "I've never slept with a woman."

She glanced up, her eyes dancing. She closed her tablet and lifted her coffee cup. "I think we both know that's a lie, counselor. Care to rephrase?"

I chuckled. "I mean that literally. I have never slept beside another person in my life."

"Oh." She frowned. "No, ah, overnight guests?"

"Never."

"Even as a kid? No sleepovers? Camping trips sharing a tent?"

"Never."

"I see."

"How long have you had problems sleeping?"

She drained her cup and stood to get another one. She lifted the carafe, one eyebrow raised in a silent question, and I held out my mug, waiting as she refilled it.

"About five years ago. I started having trouble falling asleep, then staying asleep. I would toss and turn. It drove Scott crazy, and he was very vocal about it. So, if I woke up, I would get up and go downstairs in order not to disturb him. He finally suggested I move into the guest room, saying that even my getting out of bed bothered him."

I held up my hand. "So you've been in separate rooms all this time?"

"Yes. I tried to move back, but he insisted it was better for him—that he needed to keep his mind sharp. He teased me about nocturnal visits, but of course, they never happened." She lifted one shoulder. "Frankly, it was easier. He brought so much anger to bed every night, I think it set me off and made me tense. He talked and cursed a lot in his sleep, and he thrashed a great deal. I was always worried about him kicking me. I could read if I couldn't sleep, move around."

"Did you talk to anyone?"

"I went to the doctor, but nothing short of drugging me to the max seemed to help. He suggested a therapist, but Scott refused. I gave up and accepted it. I would nap during the day and sleep a little at night..." Her voice trailed off and she sat down beside me again. "But last night was the first night in years I've had nine hours of uninterrupted sleep. I'd forgotten what it felt like to feel rested."

"I know. It's awesome." I paused. "Five years ago—so it coincided with when your marriage began to fall apart."

She paused, thinking, then nodded. "Yes, you're right. We'd been having trouble before then, but things began to go downhill fast. I was never the best of sleepers, but the worse things got, the worse my sleeping became. Separate rooms was the next step. I never put those together."

I took a long sip, letting the intense brew wash over my taste buds.

"What about you?" she asked. "How long have you had trouble sleeping?"

I stiffened. "Most of my life."

She didn't push. "I see. That must have been difficult."

I shrugged.

For a moment, she looked at me, then spoke.

"You know part of being friends is sharing, Halton. We just slept together. That was a pretty intimate thing." She tilted her head. "You asked me for honesty. Now I am asking you for the same. Talk to me."

I scrubbed my face, knowing she wasn't going to let this go. "My mother," I said shortly. "When my parents separated, she took me. She wasn't fit to be a parent. She had severe mental health issues and refused to stay on medication. I never knew what was going to happen next, and I was always on the defensive. Always bracing for the crash, the next high, or the next wave of depression. She couldn't sleep, and she kept me awake to keep her company. When she would crash, I was so worried, I couldn't sleep since I had to watch over her."

I pushed away from the island, pacing the room. "My father fought to get custody of me, but somehow, my mother always managed to pull herself together enough to win. I was a kid, and back then, no one asked the kids what they wanted. Fathers were rarely the ones wanting custody. I was torn between wanting a normal life and feeling guilty over leaving my mother. She was a master manipulator and knew exactly how to guilt me into staying. She made promises over and again—breaking them every time. She wasn't a nice person in general, so my childhood was chaotic and horrendous. My father eventually gave up and left because he couldn't stand watching it. He couldn't handle the guilt and started drinking. He died way too early, leaving me alone with her."

"Oh, Halton."

"That's what love does, Fee. It destroys. At least, it did for me. My parents both claimed to love me, yet I was the one who suffered the most neglect—all in the name of love. I never had a home or security. I had to fight tooth and nail to survive."

"Did your mother pass?"

"No, she is still kicking. She lives out west. We keep in touch via email on occasion. When she is on her meds, the tone is civil, and on occasion, there is an apology I think she might actually mean but has come far too late. When she isn't, I delete them, since she likes to blame my birth for the failure of her marriage and her health. Sadly, more are deleted than I read. Usually, I can tell from the first line. In all of them she asks for money. Never a visit or a phone call. Just money." I held up my fingers in quotation marks. "I *owe* her that at least."

I stopped in front of Fee, shocked to see her eyes glazed with tears. *Why was she crying?*

"She used the love of a child for her own selfish needs, Fee. She drained my father, then did the same for me. She warped what love should be until her way was all I knew. I broke free of her hold when I was sixteen, but it was too late. I was already twisted and jaded. From the moment I left her shadow, I was out for one person —myself."

"But you fight for children," she insisted. "For others."

I frowned. "I'm not a nice person, Fee. Fighting for others is my little bit of redemption," I confessed. "I can't love. I can't commit. I'm not a productive member of society, other than my law practice."

"You feel that is your only redemption. Fighting for others?"

"Yes."

She wiped away the tears on her cheeks with an angry swipe. "You're wrong. You don't see yourself clearly. You only allow yourself to see the negative."

"Why do you insist on seeing the good?" I retorted, crowding her. Bringing up my mother, my childhood, had dragged all the feelings I kept under lock and key to the surface. Why Fee's opinion of me mattered, I didn't understand, but one thing I did know was that it did. It mattered a great deal to me. It felt as if my life were hanging by a thread, waiting for her words.

"Because you can't. I'll be the champion for you since you're doing it for me."

Her words were barely out of her mouth, and I was kissing her. I yanked her tight to my chest and gripped her wet hair in my fist as I claimed her. There was nothing gentle about the kiss, nothing sweet and loving. It was anger and passion. Frustration and confusion.

And then, it wasn't.

Fee's arms wound around my neck, holding me close. Her touch was tender as she ran her fingers through my hair. She let me control her, my tongue demanding and hard, giving to me the entire time. Gentling my touch, I caressed the back of her neck, cradling her head in my hands. I stroked her tongue with mine, earning a low moan deep in her throat. I explored her, discovering her sweetness, reveling in her taste. Moments passed of discovery, losing myself in her, until reality roared back in when my phone rang, the sound echoing off the granite. I stepped back, meeting her wide gaze, the green verdant and startled. In an unfamiliar, tender gesture, I cupped her cheek and pressed my mouth back to hers.

"Thank you."

She smiled and covered my hand with hers.

"Back at you."

She slipped away, and I reached for my phone, shocked at my behavior, my lack of control, and the fact that I wished the damn phone hadn't interrupted us.

I was more confused than ever.

I spent the day with Fee, putting aside my confusion and, for the first time in a very long while, enjoying the free time. She insisted we stop and buy Jay a present, and his reaction to the dinosaur book she picked out was beyond enthusiastic. He sat beside her, showing her all his favorite creatures, telling her the characteristics and lifestyles. She listened to every word, asking questions and encouraging him to talk.

She had that trait down pat. She had me admit things I had never told another person.

I found everything she did fascinating, and it was difficult not to stare at her openly. Luckily, it was a sunny autumn day and the party was on their back deck, so my sunglasses hid my secret.

I noticed everything about her. The way she talked. The habit she had of flicking her hair away from her face, only to repeat the action when the long wave fell back over her shoulder. She was warm and gracious with everyone she met, shaking their hand and repeating their name. Her laugh was light and feminine, and it rang out a lot while we were there. She used her hands to gesture while she spoke. She was small in stature, but she held her head high and her presence was magnetic.

How the hell had Scott Hutchings missed all this about his wife? What the hell was he thinking, letting her go?

I had been worried things would be uncomfortable after our kiss, but she acted as though it never happened, treating me the same as she always did. My ego would have taken a blow, except I caught her more than once staring at my mouth. I had to turn away in order for her not to see my smirk. She was equally fascinated, it would seem.

I had a feeling our fascination was going to lead to some complications. I tried to decide how strongly I was going to fight it.

"So, Fee... A friend, you said?" Carl joined me on the deck.

"And a client. And right now, a temp in the office." I chuckled. "A bit of everything."

"She is lovely."

"She's having a rough time and is alone. I thought she would enjoy being with some people. I don't think dealing with my cranky ass at the office all week constitutes fun."

"You're not cranky around her."

I was at a loss for words. Something that kept happening when people brought Fee into the conversation. I recognized he was right, though. It was impossible to be cranky around her. She needed to be treated with care. She deserved that.

"She'd tell you something different, I'm sure. I like to look after my clients. Which is why I'm here," I stated pointedly.

Carl clapped me on the shoulder. "Yep. Got it." He walked away, chuckling. "This is gonna be fun." I glared at his retreating form.

What the hell was he talking about?

Fee stood, taking her tablet and empty glass with her. She had been quiet all night, reading, and I had been busy with some case notes. I tracked her with my eyes, not saying anything.

I held my breath as she paused at the edge of the living room. "Good night."

Disappointment flooded my system, but I nodded. "Night, Fee."

I heard her door shut and let my head fall back to the sofa. What did I expect? That she would ask to sleep with me again? That she'd drop her clothes and ask me to fuck her?

Last night had been a one-off. The kiss today had been an outpouring of the emotion we both experienced because of the subject matter. That was all.

It was better that way.

And maybe my body would get the message. A good night's sleep did wonders for my brain and my energy level. If I slept again tonight, perhaps I could break the cycle of insomnia once and for all.

Except, hours later, I knew I was wrong. My bed wasn't comfortable. I couldn't settle. Something was off and I couldn't decide what it was.

A noise caught my attention, and I sat up immediately. I heard the muffled sounds of footsteps and the running of water. Pushing back the blanket, I opened my door and went to the kitchen. Fee was by the sink, sipping from a glass of water. She met my eyes in the semi-dark, her green orbs worried and dull.

"Can't sleep?" I asked.

"No."

"Me either."

"I was thirsty. I thought I needed a glass of water."

"I think I know what you need."

"You do?"

I held out my hand. "Come here."

She set down her glass and came to me. Trusting and sweet, worrying her lip and hesitant, but she came. I pulled her from the kitchen and into my room. I lifted the blanket and indicated she should get in.

"I can't..."

"Just sleep, Fee. I need to see if it was a fluke." I paused. "Or if you're the difference."

Her voice was quiet in the dark. "What if I am?"

I had no answer to that question. "Please."

She slid in and I followed. It felt natural to angle toward her and tug her into my arms. Her head fit perfectly under my chin, and her closeness filled my senses with the fragrance of flowers. My body relaxed, the muscles loosening and easing. Fee sighed, snuggling closer. I held her tighter, already feeling sleep tug at my body.

"Thank you," I mumbled.

She was already out, the low clicking-purring noises starting and making me grin.

They were the last thing I heard. Sleep beckoned and I fell.

Tuesday morning, I was up early, refreshed and prepared for the week ahead. My energy level was high, and I was ready to come out swinging. I grabbed a cup of coffee and waited for Fee in the living room. She came in shortly, looking pretty. She had her hair swept up, and a simple dress swirled around her legs.

"Are you sure I should drive with you? What if Scott...?"

I shook my head, cutting off her words. "He isn't looking here for you. Besides the windows are tinted in the Mercedes. He wouldn't be able to see if it was you even if he were looking."

She picked up her purse, and I headed for the door. Her next words stopped me cold.

"Do you think I'm a whore?"

I spun around, shock making me gape. Fee clutched her purse to her chest, the grip so tight, her knuckles were white.

"Why would you ask me that question?"

"I'm still married, but I'm here with you—in your condo. In your bed. I kissed you."

I crossed the room and pulled her purse from her grip. I threw it on the sofa and clasped her hands in mine. Bending my head, I kissed her knuckles. "I'm sorry if you feel that way, Fee. That isn't how I see this at all."

"How do you see it?"

I tucked the stray wave that always bothered her behind her ear. "I don't know," I answered honestly. "I told myself I brought you here because you're my client and I had to help you. But the truth is, I wanted to bring you here. I wanted to spend a little time with you."

"Why?"

I gave her honesty because that is what I always asked of her. "Because you make me feel like a better man when you're around, Fee."

"Oh."

"I don't understand the sleeping thing. All I know is I have slept more the last three nights than I've slept in the last six months. Having you next to me is like some sort of sleeping draught. The world fades away, and I can relax." I slid my arm around her waist. "You aren't doing anything wrong, Fee. You're helping me."

"The kiss?" she whispered.

"It was just that. A kiss. Put it out of your mind. I won't cross that line again, I promise."

"How are we going to do this?"

I stepped back, gazing at her. Yesterday, we had spent together, simply doing nothing. She had read and cooked. I had worked and eaten. We had taken advantage of the rainy day and watched a movie, ending up napping on the sofa, entwined around each other once again. I couldn't remember the last time I napped. I couldn't recall feeling the way I did waking up beside her. Her drowsy smile had lit something in my chest, and I had brushed a silent kiss of thanks to her head, then slid away regretfully before I did something else.

The truth was, I wanted her. I wanted to lay her on my bed and do much more than sleep with her. I wanted to bury myself inside her—to know how she felt as she orgasmed—to hear her voice calling my name in passion. But even I wasn't enough of an asshole to do that to her. I wasn't the man for Fiona. She deserved someone who could fulfill her dreams, marry her, and give her a life filled with love. That was what she wanted and what she deserved.

But I was a big enough asshole to take what she could give me—a few moments of feeling like a better person, and some hours of unguarded rest. But it had to stop, and I had to be the one who stopped it.

"We're going to be exactly what we have been. You are my client and assistant. Nothing more, Fee," I said gently. "You know my limits. I'm going to work very hard to get your divorce pushed through fast and get you all you deserve settlement-wise. Then you're going to go and find your life."

I saw the hurt flash across her face, but she straightened her shoulders. "And you?"

I shrugged, moving farther away. "I'll carry on the way I was before. My life is set, Fee. It was set long before I met you."

"People can change."

"If they want to."

She shook her head. "You won't even try."

"Because I already know I'll fail. This is me. It's who I am." I sucked in a lungful of air, already feeling the ache my words were going to cause.

"Since you get your place tomorrow, you should stay in your own room tonight, Fee. I think it would be for the best. For both of us."

"No confusing our worlds, is what you are saying. Redrawing the lines again, Halton?"

I couldn't tell her I was already confused. And dreading the fact that I was going to go back to the fractured way I had been sleeping again. I had the feeling, without her beside me, rest was going to be even more elusive than before.

"Yes," I replied.

She picked up her purse and headed to the door. I followed close behind, hating the fact that I had hurt her but knowing there was nothing I could do about it.

ELEVEN

Halton

Although I enjoyed long weekends, the one extra day of being closed seemed to bring out a panic in people. The office was crazy all day—phone calls, emails, meetings. I wasn't due in court until Thursday, and I was grateful to have the extra time to work on my caseload.

More than once, I heard Fee's gentle voice explaining I wasn't accepting new clients at the moment and offering people names from a list I had given her. Around one, she entered my office and slid a bag onto the corner of my desk. She turned to leave, halting when I called out to her.

"What about you?"

She turned. "I have a sandwich at my desk."

I shook my head—she was still hesitant about "overstepping." I enjoyed our lunches together when I was in the office. They had, in fact, become a highlight of my day.

"Bring it in here and switch the phone to voice mail."

She carried in her sandwich and sat down, crossing her legs. "Is there a problem?"

I bit into the thick roast beef sandwich she had ordered up from the deli on the corner. I chewed and swallowed before replying.

"No. I wanted to touch base. It's been a busy day."

"It has," she murmured.

"Rene called me. He's insisting on coming on Friday for a while. He's been cleared."

"All right."

There was silence as we ate. Or rather, I ate. Fee nibbled at her sandwich, barely eating half by the time I was done mine. I balled up the paper, tossing it in the bin.

"Rene returning doesn't mean anything, Fee. You still have a place here."

"Have you ever thought of taking on a partner?" she asked. "You're busy enough to keep two or three people gainfully employed."

I sipped my cola, the cold easing the slight burn left by the horseradish on the sandwich I had inhaled. "Not really."

"Why?"

I shrugged. "I don't want a run-of-the-mill practice representing rich SOBs and divorces all the time."

"Isn't that what you're doing for me?"

I studied her. "I don't consider your case usual, or that you're an SOB."

She ignored me. "Even SOBs deserve a decent attorney. Being poor doesn't give the exclusivity to being honest or decent."

"I realize that."

"You could accomplish more with an extra body. You could still choose your cases but do even more."

"Trust would be an issue. I think having a partner would involve a lot of trust."

She rewrapped her sandwich. "Right. And you trust few people."

I narrowed my eyes, catching an undercurrent of anger in her tone. "Very few."

She stood. "Sometimes, you have to offer trust to get trust, Halton." She walked toward the door, and I was on my feet moving toward her before I could think. I caught her elbow, spinning her around.

"Hey. I do trust you."

She tried to shake off my hold, but I refused to let her move. "You wouldn't be here, working for me, if I didn't trust you. I wouldn't have had you stay in my home."

She shut her eyes, then exhaled. "I know that. I simply mean you need help. There are lots of cases you could take on that you would believe in if you had someone else working with you."

She meant more than that, but I let her go. I wasn't sure I wanted to get into the meaning of her words right now. I opened my mouth, but my private line rang, breaking the moment. I stepped back and smiled.

"I'll give it some thought. Close the door when you leave, please."

She walked past me, shutting the door. I grabbed my phone, already knowing who would be on the other end of the line. I had been waiting for this call all day, but I didn't want Fee to overhear it.

"Mr. Smithers, this is Jonas Peters of Peters, Down, and Hadley. I'm representing Scott Hutchings."

I had been wondering who he would choose. They were another firm I despised. Ambulance chasers, questionable practices, and unsavory divorces. I wasn't surprised Hutchings had chosen them to represent him. His own firm couldn't be involved. There would be a conflict of interest since part of the settlement could be their own firm.

Peters, Down, and Hadley had the same sort of scruples as Scott —in other words: none. They would be a natural choice for him. Luckily, I was much smarter than any lawyer in their firm. Scott simply hadn't accepted that fact yet.

"I've been expecting your call."

"I'd like to set up a meeting. My client is anxious to move things forward and to make this as easy as possible on all parties concerned. He was hoping we could settle all this between us without involving the courts."

I counted to ten before replying.

"How considerate of him," I responded, the sarcasm evident in my voice. "Was he thinking about making it easy on my client when he harassed her at her rented accommodations this past Friday and forced her to find another place to stay?"

"He regrets his actions. His only defense was that he became emotional when he saw the divorce papers. He overdrank and made a bad choice. We've all been there, right, Hal? I mean it was a blow to his ego. A male thing."

I blinked, unsure if this asshole was being serious or not. Was he really pulling the "*C'mon it's a guy thing—you get it*" shit on me?

"His ego," I repeated.

"Yes."

"So, if that was a blow to his ego, tell me, what did he think was going to happen after he kicked my client out of their marital home, took away her only mode of transportation, canceled her credit cards and access to their bank account, and dropped her off at a hotel like a second-rate hooker with a wave and a 'see you later'? He thought they'd have drinks and solve everything between them?"

There was a pause.

"He gave her some money."

"Again, I will refer to the second-rate hooker comment. Twenty grand for almost ten years of marriage? We both know, in Toronto, that wouldn't even cover a deposit on a place to live, Jonas. Your client handled this badly."

"He regrets his actions."

"He is going to regret it a lot more when I get through with him."

There was another pause.

"We would like to meet as soon as possible and move this forward."

Time in the world of the law has a totally different meaning. Urgent means I'll get to it when convenient. As soon as possible could be next week or next month. If a lawyer says he'll "get right back to you," grab a coffee. Maybe a sandwich. You're going to wait a while.

But I wanted this done now. I glanced at my schedule and decided to move things along fast.

"Friday afternoon. Four o'clock. My office," I snapped and hung up.

I was going to fry that bastard.

I sent a quick message to Fee telling her to move everything from three o'clock onward on Friday until next week. I sent Rene a text asking him to be here Friday afternoon. I picked up the phone and called Wyatt.

He answered after several rings, sounding distracted. In the background, I could hear a game playing. He was addicted to all that shit. Jobs like mine that paid well allowed him to spend more time playing than working. Add in pizza and beer, and his life was perfect. Normally, I found it amusing. Right now, I was annoyed.

"Put down your controller and turn off your fucking game. I need your attention."

Silence fell.

"I need everything you can find on Scott Hutchings. Attorney." I rattled off all the information I knew.

"You want finances?"

"I want it all. Finances. Where he is spending his money. Who he is spending it on. His cell phone records. I want to know what time he gets up in the morning, takes a crap, and how long he wanks off for in the shower."

There was a long pause.

"I think that is more for a PI than a job for me."

"Get me everything you can."

"Okay, I'll work on it."

"Do it fast."

"How fast? It's gonna take—"

"Fucking fast or you're fired. No more retainer. Got it?"

"Got it."

I hung up.

My mood got worse as the week progressed.

Tuesday night, Fee stayed in her room all evening, and eventually, I gave up waiting for her and went to bed. I tossed and turned all night, not even getting an hour of sleep. My bed felt strange and cold—uncomfortable.

Maybe it was time for a new mattress. I would have to look into it.

We both looked tired on Wednesday morning, but neither of us addressed the elephant in the room. I decided I would sleep better once Fee was in her own place. Having someone in my space was disturbing me. I was used to being on my own. I kept telling myself that. My world would return to normal once Fee was gone.

I ignored the laughter in my head.

Wednesday afternoon, Aiden dropped by the office and gave Fee the keys to the apartment. He perched on the edge of her desk, talking to her. For some reason, it bothered me to see his massive frame looming over her. It bothered me even more that she laughed and talked to him like an old friend. I knew he was happily married. I knew he was a friendly guy and was simply being Aiden. I didn't like it. When I heard him offer to take her to the place and show her around, I lost it.

I stormed out of my office, ignoring the fact that clients were in the waiting area. "Thanks, Aiden. I'll take it from here. I'm sure Bentley needs you back at the office. You can go. I appreciate you bringing the keys yourself."

He stood with a frown, crossing his arms. His gigantic frame dwarfed me, but I didn't back away. I met his gaze with all the anger I was feeling. He narrowed his eyes, then suddenly grinned, his eyebrows lifting as he chuckled. He stepped back, slapping me on both shoulders.

"Oh, this is awesome."

"What the hell are you on about?" I almost snarled.

Laughing, he wiped his eyes. He turned to Fee and held out his hand. "Great to meet you, Fee. No doubt, I'm going to be seeing a lot of you." He turned and headed to the door, still laughing.

He paused and met my gaze and started to laugh again. "Bent is going to howl." He walked out, pulling the door closed behind him. I glared at his retreating figure. I stomped back into my office.

"Send in the next client," I ordered, then flung myself into my chair.

What the hell was that about?

By Friday morning, I was dragging my ass. My few hours of sleep a night had turned into zero hours of sleep. Fifteen- or twenty-minute catnaps a few times during the hours of midnight and five a.m. were all I was able to manage.

And to top it off, on Wednesday night before she left my place for hers, Fee had informed me she felt it best if she came to and from the office on her own. I had argued with her, but she insisted it was for the best.

"If Scott finds that out, he will use it. If he has any idea at all that I

was ever at your place, he will twist it until it is so sordid, not even you can unsully it, Halton." She met my gaze. "I am not sure I should be here in your office, but I am enjoying the work and the challenge. I like feeling productive again—I won't allow him to take that from me as well."

"And you don't think he'll make an issue of the fact that you're living in my building?" I challenged her, unable to figure out why it was so important to me that I drive her.

She crossed her arms. "Technically, it's not your building. They have two separate addresses, Halton. I had no idea they were attached by a walkway until you told me. I doubt Scott will either. He isn't that bright."

For some reason, that made me laugh. I relaxed a little. "Come on, Fee, let me drive you."

"No. I need to do this my way."

"A cab, then. I'll arrange it for you."

"As long as you put it on Scott's bill with all the rest of the things you are covering."

Agreeing, I laughed and let it go.

For now.

I worked through Friday morning, and Rene arrived just after I broke for lunch. He looked like Rene. Dressed to the max, his head bright and gleaming, and his grin wide. I could see the effects of his accident, though. He moved a little slower, and his smile was forced at times when he turned certain ways. His arm was still in a sling and a cast, the healing wound on his head covered with a neat bandage. But his mind was sharp, and he looked happy to be back in the office. He and Fee sat together for a while and talked. He came into my office when they were done and sat across from me.

"I hear Scott is coming in this afternoon."

"Yes."

Fee had accepted the news quietly enough when I told her, but I knew she was anxious. She hid it better than I did, but I knew she wasn't sleeping either. The amount of coffee we drank in the day was staggering, but neither of us touched on the subject. It was like a landmine neither of us wanted to step on. The explosion would be deadly.

Fee walked in, interrupting us. She placed a bag and a coffee on my desk. She smiled at Rene. "Are you sure you don't want coffee? A sandwich? Anything?"

"No, dear Fee, I'm good."

"Where is your lunch?" I asked.

"I can't, Halton. Not today."

Without thinking, I grabbed her hand. "You have to eat, Fee. Something. I need you strong this afternoon."

"I'm too nervous."

I squeezed her fingers. "I'll be there with you. Every moment. He won't have a chance to be alone with you or say anything. I'll shut him down so fast, his head will spin."

Releasing her hand, I unwrapped my sandwich and rewrapped half. "Please eat this." She hesitated, and I slipped my fingers under her chin. "Please. You're too pale. You need the energy."

She met my gaze. Quietly, I added, "For me."

She took the sandwich and left. I sat down, biting into my lunch and chewing fast. It tasted like sawdust, but I needed it. I looked up to find Rene staring at me.

"What?"

He started to grin, then shook his head. "How do you want to play this?"

I took another bite, thinking. "Fee is going to be in here. I want you at your desk. Show them into the library, and I'll bring her in. She's not to be alone with him. At all."

Rene rubbed his chin. "So Fee is playing the client, I'm the worker, and you're the attorney? Those are our roles?"

"Those are the facts."

He shook his head. "There is way more to this scenario than that. You can object and deny all you want, Halton, but I know you too well."

"Deny what?"

He chuckled. "I'm going to let you figure that part out."

I slammed my hand on the desk. "I am sick of all the cryptic BS from everyone. Spit it out."

Rene studied me. "You look like shit."

"I'm not sleeping. I have a lot on my mind."

"Your client-slash-assistant looks the same way."

"She's nervous. I'm sure she's having trouble resting too. Once today is over, she'll relax."

"Uh-huh." He sat back in his chair, chuckling and muttering to himself.

I ignored him.

I heard Scott's voice outside my closed door. It annoyed me more than usual. Drawing in a long breath, I slid on my jacket, pulling down my cuffs and making sure my tie was straight. I shut my eyes and used a few relaxation mind tricks I always relied on to help center my thoughts. I needed my head clear.

I glanced at Fee. She had eaten about two bites of the sandwich I had given her. She was paler than ever, her hands fretting with the edge of her jacket and tugging on the ends of her beautiful hair. At least she wasn't chewing her nails.

I picked up her file. "Ready, Fee?"

She offered me a smile, but I saw the look in her eyes. It did something to me—tore at my chest and made me want to take away the fear in her eyes.

I didn't think, only reacted. I stepped close and pulled her into my arms. She flung her arms around my neck and buried her face into my chest. I felt the tremors that ran through her body, and I tightened my hold.

"Together, Fee. We're going to face this bastard together. He doesn't get to push you around anymore, and he doesn't determine your self-worth. You do. I do. And I think you're fucking priceless."

She glanced up at me. I cupped her face and broke my own rule. I lowered my mouth to hers and kissed her. Gently. Sweetly. Showing her, without words, how important she was.

I lifted my head and gave her a minute to gather herself. Rene opened the office door and poked his head in. He met my narrowed eyes, lifting his eyebrows a little, then nodding. He tilted his chin toward the library.

"They're ready."

I glanced down at Fee. "Okay?"

She stepped back and blew out a long breath.

"Ready."

I winked. "Okay, FeeNelly. Let's do this."

TWELVE

Fiona

Scott sat beside his lawyer, his expression fierce. I felt his anger simmering below the surface, but as instructed by Halton, I didn't engage. Halton led the way into the library, courteously pulling out my chair and waiting for me to sit before settling into the chair beside me.

"Gentlemen, thank you for agreeing to meet here."

Jonas Peters smirked. "You didn't really give us much choice, Hal."

Halton lifted one shoulder, dismissing his words. "Nonetheless. Now, let's not waste any time. I'll keep this simple. Your client asked for this divorce. My client isn't fighting his request, but we are seeking fifty percent of all marital assets, including Scott's shares in his firm."

Jonas slid a document Halton's way. "I have a signed waiver showing that Mrs. Hutchings agreed not to go after anything to do with the firm in the event they parted ways."

Halton leaned back, not at all worried. "It was signed under duress. Which I can prove." He flipped open a file. "I have medical records showing your client didn't always treat his wife with the greatest of care. Also, newer pictures from last week's assault. You might want to reconsider your options."

I lost track of the conversation after that. Scott began to curse, Jonas spoke to him quietly, then he and Halton began throwing around terms and conditions, both talking so fast, their words combined with fists being thumped on the hard, wooden table, rapid hand gestures, raised voices, and veiled threats.

It was all I could do to sit there and listen to my marriage—my life

—being reduced to this. Accusations, anger, and value. That was what it boiled down to. He said, she said. Ten years of life spread on a table filled with documents, surrounded by regret and pain. It was only Halton's presence, the feeling of his solid body beside me that kept me in my place. I could feel his warmth, his strength, and his determination as he spoke. His voice was clear and smooth. There was no hesitation on his part whether he was questioning or responding. He was in complete control, appearing almost relaxed as he presided over the meeting.

In contrast, Scott was a mass of anger across the table from me. He was red-faced and sputtering, despite his attorney's attempts to keep him calm. I felt the hatred in Scott's glare, but I refused to let him see how he affected me. I sat straight, my legs crossed, my body unconsciously angled toward Halton. Scott fidgeted, slouched, straightened, played with his tie, then slouched again. He grunted, muttered under his breath, and conferred with his attorney, often pointing his finger in my direction. Every time he did, I felt Halton's leg press against mine, his silent support appreciated.

Scott's knee bounced continuously, so much so, I wanted to say something. He ran his hand through his hair every few moments, tapped his fingers on the table, and rolled his head on his shoulders. I had never known him to be so out of control. He cleared his throat and I knew he wanted me to meet his stare. Finally, I lifted my eyes to his, dropping my gaze quickly at the wild look in his gaze. It made me shudder, and beside me, Halton shifted, subtly moving closer.

Scott stood. "I need the can."

Halton stopped mid-sentence, his eyebrows lifting at Scott's rudeness. "Through the reception area. Rene will direct you."

Jonas stood. "We're almost done, Scott."

Scott shook his head. "Now."

I frowned at the unusual conversation. Scott strode from the room, his steps hurried. He opened the door so quickly, it slammed against the wall.

Jonas stared after Scott and offered us a tight smile. "When you gotta go, you gotta go."

"So it appears."

Halton turned in my direction. "Do you need a coffee, Fee?" he asked kindly. "A water?"

"No, thank you." I leaned closer. "Is it almost over?"

He squeezed my hand, his voice low enough only I could hear him. "Yes."

Always courteous, he turned his attention to Jonas. "Anything for you? Or your client?"

Jonas shook his head, his concentration on the door. "No," he said shortly.

Halton busied himself with the papers in front of him. I watched his long fingers sort, pile, and organize them into neat batches, then he sat back, checking his watch.

"Should we check on your client?"

Before Jonas could reply, Scott walked in. He flung himself into the chair, leaning back and smirking. "Sorry."

Halton studied him intently. "Everything all right, Mr. Hutchings?"

Scott crossed his arms over his chest. "Right as rain."

For a moment, Halton tapped his pen on the file in front of him. "Fine. Let's continue."

I watched Scott, surprised by his sudden change in behavior. He was more relaxed, although his leg swung impatiently. The rest of his jerky movements had ceased.

"As I was saying, we are going to request a full audited set of all personal assets and company books and—"

"Fiona." Scott's voice was loud, interrupting Halton.

I looked across the table, meeting his eyes. The odd, angry, out-of-control gaze he focused on me caused a shiver to run down my spine. He'd had the same look in his eyes on Friday night when he had grabbed me.

"I'll give you a million. Agree, and we'll draft the papers and be done. Don't make me fight this out in court with you. I guarantee you'll lose and walk away with nothing." He glanced at Halton, loathing rolling off him. "Is that a better offer or still too second-rate hookerish, Mr. Smithers?"

Halton stood, grasping my elbow and tugging me from my chair.

"It is inappropriate is what it is, Mr. Hutchings. This meeting is over. Come with me, Fee."

Scott braced his hands on the table, spit flying as he spoke loudly. "My wife's name is Fiona. I would prefer it if you didn't manhandle her in front of me."

Halton met Scott's baleful glare. "She prefers Fee, and she's not your wife."

Scott's voice dripped with ice. "Fucking him for free legal counsel, Fiona? I hope you like sloppy seconds, Hal."

"Shut your mouth," Halton snarled. "Show Fiona some respect. She damn well deserves it."

"You wanna come and make me? God knows I would like to go a round or two with you. Mess up that pretty fucking smug face of yours."

Halton drew me back. "Rein in your client, Jonas."

He tugged me to the door as Scott stood so fast, his chair toppled over. I cringed at the loud noise and the string of expletives and threats Scott spewed toward Halton. Jonas grabbed Scott by the shoulders, talking rapidly and stopping him from moving. Rene hurried in from the front office. Halton opened the door to his office and pushed me through, turning back to the room.

"Rene, we're done." He jerked his chin toward Scott. "I'm going to cut you a break, Jonas. I'm going to pretend your client didn't say what he did or threaten me. Bring him to heel, or next time you won't be so lucky. I'll see you in court."

He shut the door firmly, turned to me, and dragged me into his arms.

Halton

Fee shook so hard, I wasn't sure how she was standing. Scott's behavior had been alarming and atrocious. When he had addressed her with his bullshit offer, I couldn't believe it. Neither could his attorney, from the shocked look on his face—we both knew his wealth exceeded that figure plus the fact that he was out of order. Scott's sudden fury had set off alarm bells in my head. Something was going on. He was erratic, angry, and clearly not thinking rationally. My one goal had been to get Fiona away from him.

I listened as Rene escorted them from the office and returned, entering my office.

"Are you both all right?"

I guided Fee to a chair, gently pushing her down. I wrapped my hands around hers, shocked at how cold her fingers felt. I rubbed them briskly.

"Scotch," I said to Rene.

He handed me a glass, and I pressed it to Fee's lips. "Sip."

She drank and swallowed, coughing as the liquor burned its way down her throat.

"One more."

She sipped, then turned her head, indicating she didn't want any more.

I tossed back the remainder of the glass, welcoming the sharp taste of the amber liquid.

"I heard everything," Rene said.

"He is out of control," I muttered.

"His eyes," Fee whispered. "Something is wrong with his eyes."

"What do you mean?" I asked. I had noticed there was something off with them, but I hadn't picked up what it was yet.

"They were black—cold. His pupils..." Her voice drifted off.

I stood. "*Fuck*. He was high. Rene, check the bathroom."

Fee frowned. "Scott doesn't do drugs."

I ran a hand through my hair. "I think you're wrong, Fee."

Rene returned. "There's some white residue on the sink."

"Lock it. I want that residue tested." I started to pace, furious. "That asshole brought coke into my place of business?" I snarled. "He got high during a consultation about his divorce? With witnesses?"

Fee looked shocked. "He always hated drugs. He rarely even drank. I don't understand."

I laid my hand on her shoulder. "I think, Fee, love, there is a lot here we don't understand. But I'm going to find out."

Rene stared at me, shock registering on his face. I frowned at him, unsure why he was looking at me that way. I ignored him, crossed to my desk, and picked up the phone, dialing the number I swore I wouldn't use again.

"Reid Matthews."

"Reid, it's Hal."

"You have Wyatt," he reminded me dryly.

"I need you. I need your skills. Name your price."

He sighed. "You clear it with Bentley first. I'm not jeopardizing my future, Hal."

"You don't have to. I want you to work with Wyatt—make sure he's looking in the right places. Direct him. I need this." I glanced at Fee, meeting her worried eyes. I swung my chair around to avoid Rene's piercing stare. I dropped my voice. "It's personal, Reid. It's—" I swallowed "—it's important."

"Tell me."

Rene left and Fee sat in the library. After a long phone call with Bentley and another with Aiden, I waited for the technician Aiden promised to send over. Tom arrived, took pictures, samples, and documented not only the bathroom but the chair Scott had sat in and the area around him.

"Residual dust," he explained. "In case."

After he left, I closed the office and drove Fee home. She didn't object this time. Nor did she say a word when I walked her to her door and waited until she walked in. I followed, giving the place a quick inspection. It was small, but well appointed, clean, and above all, safe.

I turned to Fee. "Are you all right?"

"I'm fine."

I laughed and shook my head. "I don't know much about women, but I do know the word fine means anything but."

She passed a hand over her head, the silver glinting in the light. "I'm a little shaken. If what you suspect is right...what does that mean?"

I shrugged. "It depends on their next move. If he has a drug habit, it might explain his sloppy handling of everything. It might work in our favor since his attorney won't want it known what is happening. Or Scott, being Scott, might go off the rails and make his life hell. Either way, I'll handle it. I'm going to go ahead and try to get the document you signed struck down, then we'll decide our next step." I paused. "Or if you want, I can call Jonas and tell him you'll take the one million, plus Scott pays my bill, and it's done."

I saw her indecision. "Hey," I murmured. "If this is too much, say it and I'll make it happen."

"What would you do?"

I shook my head. "I can't, Fee. I can't tell you what to do. I'm not you."

She frowned, rubbing her arms.

"Think about it," I encouraged. "Do you want me to stay?"

Her gaze lingered on the window and the gathering storm clouds. "No, I need to be alone. To think."

It made sense, yet I was loath to leave her. She seemed jittery—more than I would have expected, even after the tumultuous afternoon.

"Are you staying in tonight?"

"Yes."

"You'll eat?"

The glass rattled in the windows as the wind picked up. Fee grimaced, her fingers twisting with nerves. "I'll try."

"Fee, what is it?" I stepped closer. "What is making you so anxious? It's more than what happened earlier."

"I hate storms," she confessed, her eyes flickering toward the windows again. "I know it sounds silly, but I'm terrified of them."

I laid my hand on her arm. "It's not silly. Everyone has fears."

"Scott used to laugh at me."

"As we have established, Scott is an asshole."

She giggled, her eyes wide as if shocked at her reaction.

"He wasn't always an asshole."

"Neither was I. We change."

This time, she touched me, cupping my cheek. "No, Halton, you're not an asshole. Blunt, direct, and arrogant, but not an asshole."

I covered her hand with mine. "I don't like storms either." I drew in a deep breath, sharing something personal with her. "When I was a kid, my mother forgot about me one day. She took me to the park and just...forgot. She went home and left me, and a storm hit. I was all alone in the park, scared shitless."

"Oh, Halton."

"A neighbor was driving by and saw me huddled under a tree. He picked me up and took me home. She answered the door, shocked to see me. She thought I was in my room, playing." I shrugged. "It was one of many times. But from then on, I hated storms too."

Our gazes locked. Understanding shone in her green eyes. It was strangely comforting.

"Do you want me to stay for a while, Fee? Ride out the storm together?"

"I don't want to be a bother."

I huffed and shrugged off my jacket. "You know what? I'm starving. I'll order food, and we can eat. I'll leave once the worst is over. We'll both feel better. Okay?" I met her gaze, imploring her silently to agree. To accept this small gesture from me.

"Okay," she agreed. "I would like the company."

"Great."

Fee surprised me and ate the dinner I ordered. She had a bottle of wine in the fridge, and I poured us each a large glass, encouraging her to drink while we waited for the Chinese food to arrive. It helped her relax, and she actually laughed at some of the silly stories I told her of odd cases I had handled over the years. I tried to divert her attention from the storm raging outside, even going so far as to play cards with her.

I couldn't remember the last time I had played cards. I discovered a competitive streak in Fee. She made me laugh when she would change the rules to suit herself, and more than once, I caught her peeking at cards in order to win. I was certain Go Fish had never been played as aggressively as it was between us.

I couldn't remember the last time I enjoyed an evening so much. Despite the weather and the reason I was there with her, I liked it.

Once the storm calmed and I could see she was tiring, I picked up my jacket, slinging it over my shoulder. I stood in her doorway, hesitating.

"It's going to be okay, Fee."

"I know," she stated simply.

"Really?" I asked, surprised.

She nodded. "I have Hal Smithers on my side."

Without thought, I wrapped a hand around her waist and drew her close. I leaned down and brushed my mouth over hers. "Yes, FeeNelly, you do."

She cupped my cheek, and our eyes locked. The air around us sizzled with the tension. I could feel her breath on my face, light puffs of air that drifted over my skin. She moved her fingers restlessly on my skin, and I tightened mine on her hip. One small dip and my mouth would be on hers again. That was all it would take. I cleared my throat, knowing there was a line I didn't dare cross.

"If things get scary again, call me. I can be here in five minutes," I told her, my voice husky.

"Thank you."

Then she leaned up and kissed me.

Hours later, I was still pacing. There would be no sleep for me tonight, and I hadn't even bothered trying. My mind was racing, my body tense. All I could think about was Fee. The way she felt in my arms. The taste of her when her lips were against mine. How her heat had soaked into my skin, warming me, her scent surrounding us.

The kiss had been sweet, brief, and fucking shattered my mind.

I had left immediately. It was either walk out the door, or I'd have her on the bed in the small apartment, naked and pleading in five minutes.

Jesus, I was still hard.

I wanted her on so many levels, I couldn't even separate them.

Physically, my draw to her had grown. Morphed and intensified. I realized how often I watched her. Listened to her. I knew where she was in the office every moment I was there with her.

And she was fucking everywhere.

I sat on the edge of my bed, holding my head in my hands.

How had this happened?

Fee was a client. That was all she was supposed to be.

But there was something—a sense of *more* with her. I didn't understand it.

I didn't like it.

My phone buzzed and I grabbed it.

Fee: I'm sorry. I shouldn't have kissed you.
Hal: I'm not sorry—and for that, I *am* sorry.
Fee: You're twisting your words, counselor.
Hal: It's what I'm good at.
Fee: You're good at much more than you give yourself credit for.
Hal: If you knew how much I wanted to show you how good I am, you would fire me and walk.
Fee: I don't want to fire you, but I have a question.
Hal: Ask me.
Fee: Do you want me because it would piss off Scott?
Hal: This has nothing to do with Scott. How I feel has everything to do with you, Fee. It's all you.

I paused, then added, **And it fucking scares me.**

Fee: Would it help if I told you I felt it too and I don't understand it?
Hal: Yeah, FeeNelly, that helps. But we can't. It's that simple.

She didn't respond.

Hal: It's late. You should sleep.
Fee: The last time I slept was in your arms.

I groaned, dropping my head, thinking of how I slept beside her. How great it felt to rest and wake up beside her soft body.

Hal: Fee, if you were in my bed, I promise you, sleep would have to wait. For a long time.

It took a few moments for her reply to appear.

Fee: I would be okay with that.
Hal: We can't, Fee. You deserve so much more than me.
You deserve the world. I'm not a forever kind of guy.
I'm Mr. In the Moment.
Fee: I know. Goodnight, Halton.
Hal: Goodnight, Fee.

I tossed my phone beside me and flopped back on the mattress. I stared at the ceiling, unable to stop thinking about her. With me. Under me. Tucked beside me. Buried inside her. Listening to her laugh and being able to touch her the way I wanted. Everywhere.

I ran my hand over my eyes and scrubbed at my beard. I slid my hand down my chest to my aching cock. But it wasn't right. It wasn't my hand I wanted.

My phone buzzed, and I looked at the screen.

Fee: Maybe I want to live in the moment.

Then I heard the knock on my door.

Fiona

Halton flung open his door, his gaze intense. Bare-chested, black boxers hugging his hips and showing off his impressive bulge, he was sexy, stern, and barely hanging on to his control. He curled his hand around the door, his grip so tight, his knuckles were white. His breathing was labored, his chest rising and falling in rapid succession. He pinned me with his eyes, so dark, they were almost black.

"You might regret this."

I shook my head, trying not to let him see how hard I was shaking. "No, I won't."

"How can you be sure?"

I lifted my chin. "Because I'm making the decision. For me. Only me."

"I can't give you what you want, Fee."

"Right now, I want you."

He released the door and grabbed me, dragging me into his condo. In seconds, my coat was pushed off my shoulders, leaving me in my tank top and cotton sleep pants. I hadn't even bothered to change, not giving myself time to talk myself out of this. He lifted me into his arms, cupping my ass, wrapping my legs around his waist. His cock, his thick, massive cock, ground against my core, making me whimper. His mouth was hard, possessive, claiming. He kissed me as if he were a dying man and I was his oxygen. He stroked his tongue over mine, sliding it in deep, his taste consuming me. He buried his hand into my hair, yanking the clip loose and tossing it over his shoulder. I heard the sound of it hitting the wall as he wound his fist into my hair, tugging my head back and licking and biting his way down my throat over the juncture of my neck.

"Now," he growled. "Tell me to stop now. It's the only time I can try, Fee."

"No," I replied, desperate and needy. "I want you, Halton. More than I've ever wanted anyone." I grabbed his face and met his eyes, needing him to understand. "*Anyone.*"

"Oh, you got me, love." He covered my mouth and carried me down the hall, his hands roaming over my back, cupping my ass, burrowing under my tank top, running his fingers over my spine. "I'm going to fuck you well, baby. So well, you'll forget there has ever been anyone else."

He lowered me to the mattress, his body following me down to the plush cushion. Moments passed of just our mouths—kissing, tasting, and learning. Then he pushed back, looming over me.

"I want you naked."

I was shy as he eased down my pants, then urged me up and tugged away my tank top. He laid me back down, rested his palms on my thighs, and stared. Lifting his hand, he traced over my collarbone, down my chest, drifting his fingers over my breasts, causing my nipples to peak.

"You are the most beautiful woman I have ever seen," he murmured.

I blushed, not meeting his eyes.

"Hey," he called, waiting until I lifted my eyes to his. "You know my rule. Honesty. I wouldn't say it unless I meant it. You are exquisite, Fee."

Truth blazed from his eyes. I warmed under his frank stare, his desire for me obvious. Using his thumbs, he drew small circles on my thighs, increasing the pressure until I sighed and opened my legs.

He widened his caresses, slowly edging toward my pussy, his thumbs finally brushing against the curls. I whimpered as he spread me wide, my breathing becoming frantic as he lowered his head and caressed me with his mouth, the gentleness of his lips almost reverent.

"Exquisite," he repeated.

Then he attacked.

He dragged his tongue up my slit, swirling it around my clit, making me arch off the bed. Gasping, I grabbed at his hair, yanking, pulling, pushing. He lapped at me and slid one long finger inside, never stopping the magic his tongue was creating. I cried out as he added another finger, stroking me in a place I never knew existed. Pleasure, hot and intense, spiked and I came. Sudden, hard, and screaming. He never wavered, riding out my orgasm and pushing me open wider, doing things with his tongue I was certain were illegal in many countries. He slid one finger to my ass, using my own wetness to ease inside.

Still reeling from my orgasm, I gasped at the feeling. He raised his head, licking his lips. "You like that, baby? You like my finger in your ass?"

"Oh God," I whispered. "Halton, please," I begged.

For what, I wasn't sure, but he knew.

"I'll take care of you," he promised.

He nuzzled my pussy, lapping long and slow. "Jesus, you are so delicious. I'm never going to get my fill of this. Of you."

He rose and spread my legs wide, settling between them. He made quick work of a condom then he dragged the heavy head of his cock along my folds. Over and again. He grabbed my head, lifting it to his, kissing me. He tasted of me, that fact somehow turning me on even more.

Then he slammed into me. I cried out into his mouth as he began to move.

Hard. Long strokes of his cock, withdrawing almost to the end, then driving back into me. His hips circled, his thrusts deep and steady. He kissed my face, my neck, sucked on my nipples until they were red and glistening from his mouth. He groaned and cursed. Breathed my name like a prayer. Sweat beaded on his forehead, and his muscles bunched and rippled under his skin.

With a low growl, he pulled out, sliding his hands under my back. Effortlessly, he turned me over.

"On your knees, Fee. *Now*. Show me your ass."

I did as he asked, crying out when he slid back inside, the depth of his penetration shocking. I had never felt so full, so taken, so used, and yet so desired, so *sexy*, until this moment. Halton gripped my hips, driving into me. He slid his big hands under my chest, tweaking and pulling at my nipples until they were hard and throbbing.

My skin grew damp, and he lifted me suddenly, settling me on his lap. His chest rubbed against the slope of my back, the rough hairs dragging along my skin. He thrust up hard, biting and licking at my neck, then wrapped my hair in his hand, tilted my head and covered my mouth, kissing me hard.

"Gonna come, Fee. I want you to come with me," he grunted. "Fuck, baby, *now*. Please come now."

He pressed his fingers to my clit and applied the pressure exactly where I needed him.

I exploded, my pussy clamping down on him, milking him as he released, shaking, groaning, and calling my name.

He stilled, wrapping his arms around me and holding me close. His mouth that had been hard and demanding became soft. Gentle. Tiny kisses on my neck. Small tugs on my lobe. Sweeping passes along my cheek and lips. He eased me to the mattress and rubbed my legs. He left for a moment, then returned, slipping into the bed beside me. He tugged me to his chest, pressing his mouth to my forehead.

"Okay, love?"

I glanced up at him in the semidarkness. "You keep calling me that."

"Calling you what?"

"Love."

He looked surprised. "I wasn't even aware I did it," he mused.

"I like it."

"It doesn't mean..." His voice drifted off, and he sighed. "It means you're special, Fee. But special isn't forever."

I snuggled into his arms. "I know. But this, tonight, will forever be special to me."

The room was silent, and I felt sleep taking me. Just before I succumbed, I heard his voice.

"For me too."

THIRTEEN

Halton

I lay in the dim light of early morning, my body rested, my mind wide awake. Fee was snuggled as tight as possible. I had my arm around her, holding her close, my leg trapped between hers. Her head rested on my shoulder, her silky hair a messy nest from my hands. I'd had her again in the night, and I knew as soon as she stirred, I would take her once more.

I craved her. Her body. Her closeness. I didn't understand it, and right now, I didn't want to question it. I simply wanted to take Fee's words and live them.

"Right now, I want you."

I stroked her silky tresses, running the strands between my fingers. I found her hair fascinating. And sexy. The youthful beauty of her face was highlighted by the silver-gray coloring of her hair. It emphasized the vivid green of her eyes, the variance giving her a unique look I found very attractive. Add in the beauty I knew her soul to contain and she was exceptional.

Scott Hutchings was more of an idiot than I had ever guessed.

I looked down at her as she slept. The passion we shared last night had been explosive. She was giving, responsive, and vocal once she forgot her shyness. She had whispered that her love life with Scott hadn't been very good, and I had assured her more than once it was on him. She was incredible. There was no other word for it. How he had ignored her for four years and cheated on this woman was beyond me.

I had broken every rule I had with Fee. I had slept with a client. An employee. A person struggling and vulnerable. I had taken advantage of that fact. Rene would kill me if he found out—he had taken a strong liking to Fee, and I knew he felt quite protective of her.

"Stop," Fee's groggy voice murmured.

I dropped my chin to peer at her. Green eyes, warm and concerned, returned my gaze.

"What?"

"I can feel your guilt, Halton. You didn't do anything. I wanted this. I wanted you." She huffed out a sigh. "I pushed this, not you."

I stroked her cheek. "I didn't resist too hard, Fee. I wanted you too much."

"I know this is complicated, Halton. But can't we set some ground rules and try?"

"Try what, exactly?" I asked, my nerves tight.

What was she going to ask me?

She pushed her hair off her shoulder, huffing in annoyance as one long wave fell back. I tucked it behind her ear.

"Tell me."

"Can't we be attorney and client when we have to be, boss and employee during the day, and just Fee and Halton at other times?"

"That's a lot of hats to wear, Fee. I worry—"

She shook her head, interrupting me. "I know your boundaries, Halton. I'm not asking anything of you. You don't want a relationship. You don't believe in them. I heard you, and I'm not asking you for anything more than you can give. I want this for now, not forever."

A strange sensation shook me. It felt almost like hurt. But why should I be hurt? I had a beautiful woman in my bed assuring me she wanted nothing from me but what I was willing to give. It was a dream come true.

Oddly, it felt more like a nightmare.

But I heard her words loud and clear, and I forced a smile to my face, shoving aside the confusing thoughts. "So, you're saying you just want me for sex, Fee?"

She flushed, the color spreading across her cheeks. "No, ah, I—"

She gasped as I rolled us over, settling between her spread legs. "I hear you, Fee. We can wear as many hats as you want right now." I hovered over her, dragging the blunt head of my cock against her. She moaned low in her throat.

"Speaking of hats right now..." I growled and reached into the drawer for a condom.

Laughing, she arched, sliding her arms around my neck and drawing me down to her mouth. "Take me, Halton."

"Oh baby, you don't have to ask twice."

Fee accompanied me to my weekly Dads Seeking Justice meeting. Rene had been with me a few times, but she was the first woman who had ever been present. At first, I was worried they would be uncomfortable with her presence, but she laid my fears to rest quickly, weaving her magic with them all. She sat beside me, taking notes, and even made suggestions to a few of the men there. Her warmth and empathy were hard to resist, and by the end of the meeting, they were enamored of her. In fact, I thought a couple of them were too enamored, and I glared, staying close to her as they made a point of talking to her. Finally fed up, I slid an arm around her waist.

"We should head home, Fee. We have plans for later."

She blinked at me, her cheeks flushing a little, then nodded.

"Gentlemen," I smirked, tightening my grip. "I'll see you next week."

I felt their stares as I led her to the car, opening the door and waiting for her to slide in. I waved nonchalantly at them as I crossed to the driver's seat and got in beside her.

Fee glanced at me, a grin tugging at her mouth. "Was that necessary?"

I clicked my seat belt in place and shifted into drive. "Very."

Her grin became a full-blown smile. "Okay, then. And what, exactly, are these plans?"

"I plan to fuck you when we get home," I growled. "A lot. You on board with that?"

Turning in her seat, she slid her hand up my thigh, squeezing my cock, which was already hard from me only thinking about her under me again. "Totally," she murmured.

"Good." I pressed on the accelerator. "Lunch, then my bed. All afternoon."

She stroked my erection. "Maybe we need to order in. And start in the living room."

The thought of her bent over the back of my sofa was too much. I tossed her my phone. "Pick whatever you want. Make it full of protein. You're going to need it."

She leaned her head back, her gorgeous eyes filled with mischief. "Sounds like I'm going to be full of you."

I grabbed her hand and lifted it to my mouth, kissing her knuckles. "All day, love. All day."

I held her hand the rest of the way home.

I pulled her into the condo as soon as we arrived, walking her backward to the sofa, our mouths fused together, my tongue deep and claiming. I had never really liked kissing before Fee. It was just a means to an end, the brief pressing of my mouth to theirs, a need to control them with no emotion or need behind it.

But with Fee, it was vital. Pleasurable. The way her lips moved with mine. The feel of her tongue stroking along my mouth, running along my teeth, and twisting around mine sent me reeling. Her taste was an aphrodisiac, and I couldn't get enough of it. Of her.

Yanking my shirt over my head, I hoisted her to the back of the sofa, wrapping her legs around my waist, keeping her pinned tight to my chest. I ground against her, pulling up the back of her shirt and running my hands over her smooth skin, smiling against her mouth at the shivers I felt. She was so damn responsive. I broke away from her, tugging her sweater from her shoulders and lifting her shirt over her head and tossing it to the side. Her small, perfect breasts fit into my hands as if they were made for me. Her nipples were hard buds against the callused skin of my palms.

"No bra, baby?" I grinned. "How convenient."

She lifted one shoulder. "I never wear one on the weekend. I don't really need it." She glanced down. "Scott wanted me to get a boob job, but—"

I silenced her with a finger pressed to her lips. "I never want to hear his name while we're together like this. What he liked or wanted doesn't matter anymore."

"But this does?" she asked, her trembling voice showing her anxiety to my response.

I had to give her the truth. "Yeah, it does."

How, I didn't understand, but I knew that it did. For both of us.

I pulled her off the sofa, sliding her pants down her legs, once again caught in her beauty. She was perfectly proportioned. Delicate but curvy, with an indented waist and rounded hips. Her legs were slender with shapely calves. She had tiny feet, and her toenails were painted a bright pink. Her hair was up today, tendrils escaping around her face. Her lips were red and swollen from mine, the flush on her cheeks spreading to her chest. I lowered my head, tracing her collarbone with my mouth and teasing the nipples of her perky, perfect tits with my tongue and fingers. I lifted her, pushing her legs apart and kneeling in front of her. Her pussy glistened, her legs trembling as I pressed closer, sliding my tongue along her folds. She gripped my hair, her head falling back as she moaned. I grasped her knees, pushing them apart, then grabbed her ass and dragged her closer to my mouth. I ravished her. Licking. Biting. Sucking. Driving her to the edge then pulling back, ramping up her desire until she was crying out, her fingers buried in my hair, her legs wrapped around my head and her voice getting louder. She came, her honey flooding my mouth, her body shaking and tense.

My cock pressed against my zipper, desperate and aching. I needed her more than I could ever remember needing anything. Anyone.

I fumbled with my belt buckle, pushing my jeans down as I stood. In one frantic thrust, I was inside her, fucking her hard. She wrapped her arms around my neck, holding tight as I took her. Frenzied. Grasping. Gripping her hips and slamming into her. She dug her nails into my back and I hissed at the flash of pain.

"More," I demanded, flinging her leg over my arm and sinking deeper into her.

She cried out and clutched at my hair, gripping my bicep in order to hold on. Sweat poured down my back. Her nipples, hard little pebbles, rubbed against the coarse hair on my chest. I grunted and cursed, chasing the orgasm building within me. She whimpered, arching and meeting my thrusts, pleading and begging. She gasped when I pulled out, flipping and lifting her over the back of the sofa and sinking into her from behind, the angle deep and mind-blowing. She was hot, wet, and so tight around my cock, it was strangling me. I fucking loved it.

I wrapped an arm around her waist, anchoring her to me. I

dropped my face to her neck, licking and biting her skin, whispering all the dirty thoughts I had into her ear.

"You are so fucking tight, Fee."

"You like this angle, baby? You like me taking you like this?"

"I want you to come all over my cock, Fee. Drench me."

I slid my hand under her and pressed on her clit. Her bud was as hard for me as my cock was for her. It was what she needed. She spasmed, her orgasm hitting her hard. She cried out, my name falling from her lips as her pussy clamped down on my cock.

Ecstasy hit like a tsunami, engulfing me—obliterating everything in its path. I came hard, gripping her fiercely, growling her name and riding out the intense sensations with my head resting on the nape of her neck, my mouth pressed to her skin, and my cock buried in her heat.

Moments passed before I could lift myself away from her. I pressed long kisses along the ridge of her spine, easing myself away. I ran my hands along her back, stroking the soft skin of her shoulders. "Okay, love?" I asked, helping her to straighten. She sighed, leaning back into me, and I wrapped my arm around her waist, feeling the aftermath of her shivers. I pulled the hair away from her face—at some point I had yanked out her hair clip—and pressed a kiss to her neck.

"Fee?" I asked, worried. I had lost myself with her, forgetting how small and delicate she was. "Are you okay?"

"Mm-hmm," she murmured, leaning into me.

I chuckled. "Did I fuck all the words out of you?"

She giggled, her hand drifting up to cup my cheek. "I think so." She turned, facing me. "I need to go get cleaned up. You made a mess."

I began to chuckle, then froze as the reality of her words hit me.

I hadn't used a condom. No wonder I had been in such a frenzy and she had felt so fucking good.

Without a word, I picked her up and rushed down the hall. In the shower, I turned the water as hot as I thought she could take and pushed her onto the shower bench. "Open up, Fee," I commanded, grabbing the handheld unit and directing the water at her. "I need to get this out of you."

I knew I was acting irrationally, but I couldn't stop myself. "There's a pill, right?" I demanded. "A pill you can take in case I got you pregnant?"

She gazed up at me, scared and confused.

"I forgot, Fee. I forgot a condom. I swear to you I'm clean, but I—"

She stilled my hand and shook her head. "I'm clean too, Halton. And I can't get pregnant."

"What?"

"We tried early on in our marriage. And again later. Nothing happened. Scott was tested, and the results showed he was fine. More than fine—his sperm were active and fertile. The tests concluded it was me. We never conceived. Another way I failed him." Her voice shook. "It was best, considering how it has ended anyway." She cleared her throat. "I can't get pregnant, so you're fine. We're fine," she assured me, her eyes luminous with tears. "I need you to calm down, please."

I sank to my knees in front of her, cupping her face, the steam billowing around us. I recalled her saying they never had kids, but she never explained it further. For some reason, my heart broke at the sadness in her eyes.

"You would have been an incredible mother," I murmured. "But you didn't fail him, Fee. He failed you on so many levels." I didn't add I was glad she didn't have any kids—not because of how I felt about them—but because I didn't want her attached to him in any way.

"I guess, in the end, we failed each other."

I shook my head in disbelief. No matter how much of an asshole he was, no matter how badly he had hurt her, she was unable not to include herself in the blame.

I pressed a kiss to her mouth. "I'm sorry, Fee. I overreacted."

She stood, picking up the shower head from the floor. She ran it over my shoulders, the heat hitting the small scrapes left by her nails.

I hissed at the sensation but somehow enjoyed it, knowing she marked me.

"Stand up, Halton. Let's get clean. We can get dirty together again later."

I stood and took the shower head from her. I caught her in my arms and kissed her. I kissed her for many reasons. For the incredible sex. For the way she soothed me. For not getting upset at my overreaction. For the pain she had suffered because of Scott, and for the bad memory I had brought to life because of my carelessness.

I kissed her because I wanted to.

Because she was Fee.

We finally ate the lunch we had dropped by the door, and the rest of the day was quiet. Fee was more withdrawn than I was used to, and I blamed myself and my reaction earlier. I had spoiled an incredibly epic sexual moment for us. Still, she smiled and responded when I spoke to her, laughed in amusement as I read her one of Rene's funny texts about being held prisoner again, and asked me some more questions about Dads Seeking Justice.

"Do you ever help women—the mothers who are getting screwed over?"

"Yes. All the time." I scrubbed my face. "I volunteer with the group because it seemed there were fewer lawyers wanting to help the fathers. I also volunteer at a group for women, but there are more lawyers willing to put forth the effort there. So I spend more time with the dads group. If I'm needed at the other, I go there or the women can come to me. All free, of course."

She didn't meet my eyes as she shook her head.

"What?"

She lifted her shoulders. "I think you're remarkable. But if I say that, you'll make some offhand remark to disagree with me, so I will keep my opinion to myself."

I chuckled because she was right. Except...

"I like knowing you think highly of me, Fee. I admit I don't think I deserve it, but I like it," I confessed.

"You really believe you are an asshole."

I remained silent.

"Scott is an asshole," she stated. "He treats people terribly. You treat people, even the lawyers you go up against, with respect. Scott doesn't know the meaning of the word. Fighting for your clients, living your life with no apologies, doesn't mean you're an asshole, Halton."

I had no words to offer her. At times, her quiet observations astounded me.

She laid her cheek on her hand, studying me. "Why you think you're such a terrible person, I don't know. I think there is good in everyone." She sighed quietly. "In fact, I'd go as far as to say, there is a little bit of perfection in everyone."

I arched my eyebrow at her and tapped her foot with mine. "I think you're being a little sentimental. I mean, *everyone*?" I asked pointedly. I knew I had no perfection within me, and I knew, without a doubt, her ex didn't either.

She glanced out the window, wistful and pensive. "I like to think the man I fell in love with, the one who was still young enough to believe, and promised to love me forever, was real. That deep inside, he was good. That his aspirations to *do* good were his bit of perfection."

"What do you think happened?"

"He grew up. He listened to the wrong people and he became the very thing he wanted to fight against. And somewhere along the way, he lost the goodness. And his love for me, I suppose."

The words were out before I could stop them. "Then he lost everything."

She tapped my foot and grinned. "Now who's being sentimental?"

"Quiet. You tell anyone, I'll deny it ever happened. I'm good at that, you know."

She lifted her tablet, trying to hide her amusement. "Duly noted, counselor."

Fee spent the rest of the afternoon on the sofa, reading, sipping tea, and at times, staring out the window. I worked on some notes, went through my schedule, and finally kicked back with a book and a glass of wine, enjoying her silent company. I couldn't recall ever spending this much time with a woman before, simply being. It felt strange, yet I liked it.

I noticed her eyes drifting shut, and I rearranged myself on the sofa, patting my chest. "Got a spot for you, Fee."

She slid next to me, burrowing close. She liked to be held as she slept. It was her trigger, the way the feel of her against me was mine. I tried to concentrate on my book but gave up and ran my hand through her hair in a repetitive motion, knowing the moment she was asleep. I set aside my book and studied her briefly, watching the steady rise and fall of her chest, listening to her odd clicking-purring noises. Once again, they reminded me of something, but I couldn't place it. I shut my eyes and enjoyed the warmth of her, the mysteriously comforting sounds of her noises, and I slept.

After our nap, Fee made sandwiches, while I grabbed some cold beer and found the chips I had in the cupboard.

"There's a *Jurassic Park* marathon on tonight," I informed her.

"Um, yay?" she mumbled, adding another sandwich to the pile.

"We need more than those," I informed her.

"How on earth do you consume the amount of food you do and still look like—" she indicated my form with a wave of her fingers "—that?"

I sidled up behind her, wrapping my arms around her waist and nipping her neck. "You like how I look, Fee?" I slid my hands under the loose shirt she wore, skimming my fingers along the supple skin of her stomach. She shivered, making me grin. I enjoyed her reactions. I tugged on her earlobe. "Do you?"

"Yes," she whispered breathlessly.

"Good. The feeling is mutual. I think you're the sexiest woman I've ever seen."

She stilled. "Don't."

"Don't what?"

"Don't feed me lines. I prefer your honesty."

Frowning, I spun her around and gripped her chin. "I am telling the truth, Fee. You are the whole package. Sweet, sexy, and smart. All of it. That's exactly what I think. You want to challenge me on that?"

She pursed her lips in disbelief, and I shook my head. "Well, I have no choice but to prove it." She gasped as I lifted her to the counter, pushing away the sandwiches she was making.

"What are you doing?"

I yanked down her yoga pants. "Proving my case."

"Oh." She inhaled hard as I dipped my fingers between her legs. "*Oh.*"

I pulled her toward the edge, pushing her legs open wider. I crouched in front of her. "I have quite the closing argument. You ready to hear it?"

"Oh God, *yes.*"

I kissed her thigh, tracing my tongue up her leg. "Hold tight, Fee. It's a long one."

"That's it!" I yelled, grabbing the remote.

Fee looked at me, startled. "What's it?"

I backed up the movie. "Listen."

She frowned. "What am I listening to?"

"The odd clicking-purring noise thing the velociraptor is making. I knew I had heard it before." I grinned at her. "It's you."

"Excuse me?"

"You make the funniest little noise when you sleep. You sound like a raptor. Muted and much less dangerous, of course, but that's what you sound like."

"They screech and tear people apart with their long claws!" she gasped.

I laughed. "They also make a funny clicking-purring noise at times. That's the one I'm talking about."

She made me play it again, and she giggled. "You know, my roommate at university told me I made odd noises."

I nodded sagely. "You do. It's quite amusing."

Fee rolled her eyes and continued. "But she never compared me to a dinosaur—especially a scary one. I think you're a little rude."

"I'll apologize, but it's true. You sound exactly like that."

"Hmph," she replied, tilting her head as if offended.

I nudged her playfully. "I think you're the cutest raptor I've ever seen, though."

"Nice try."

"I'll give you the last brownie?" I asked, handing her the plate. She had whipped them up this afternoon, and they were awesome. I was hoping she would refuse, but she took it.

"Hardly a grand gesture, Halton. There are more in the kitchen."

I rubbed my chin. "I'll let you snuggle closer when more scary parts happen." She had never seen the movies—something that shocked me and I was determined to change tonight.

"I want popcorn."

I leaned over and kissed her. "Your wish is my command, FeeNellyRaptor."

Her laughter made me grin all the way to the kitchen.

It was late when the marathon was over. Fee stood, taking the dirty dishes to the kitchen and loading them in the dishwasher. I followed after shutting down the entertainment system.

She wiped her hands on the dish towel, then hesitated.

"Well, I guess I should, ah, go?"

"Go?"

"Home," she clarified.

I shook my head. "Stay." I inhaled and held out my hand. "Please."

I led her to my room and let her get ready for bed, loaning her a T-shirt. She slid in beside me and I pulled her close, breathing in her scent.

I shut off the light, the darkness surrounding us. She nestled close, and I pressed a kiss to the top of her head. We were silent for a few moments, then I spoke.

"Fee..."

She tilted back her head, looking at me in the dark. "What is it?"

I had to tell her. "Earlier today, after the sofa, when I..."

"Freaked out?" she finished for me.

"Yeah," I admitted. "My reaction—the way I feel—it isn't about you, okay? I need you to understand that."

"What is it about, Halton?"

I sighed, finding her hand in the dark and kissing her knuckles before resting our clasped palms on my chest.

"My mother had severe mental issues. My father drank himself to death at an early age. I'm an emotional vacuum, Fee. There's nothing there. I don't want to pass that sort of DNA along to some innocent child."

She was silent, only the press of her hand in mine and her sigh letting me know she was listening.

"I have nothing to offer anyone aside from material things, Fee. And to be honest, I'm too selfish to want to share those. I had to work hard to get them, and I have no desire to lose any of them to someone who would walk away."

"You think so little of yourself, you don't think anyone would love you enough to stay, Halton."

Her words were a statement, not a question.

152

"I know myself—that's all."

She sighed and leaned up, pressing her lips to mine. Her touch was gentle, her voice tender when she spoke.

"I think you're wrong, Halton. I think you have hidden parts of yourself away—even from your own mind. You are such an amazing man."

I slid my hand up her neck, pressing her toward to my mouth. "You're the wrong one, Fee. But thank you for thinking of me in such a way."

Her whimper spurred me on. I couldn't give her what she deserved, but I could give her pleasure.

We kissed endlessly. Slow, lazy kisses. Languid glides of our tongues that teased and touched. They deepened slowly, our breathing becoming deep and harsh. I tugged away the T-shirt with eager fingers, pressing her into my mattress. I hovered over her, nestled between her legs.

"Just me, Fee?" I rasped, dragging my cock along her wetness. "Can I have you again with nothing between us?"

She wrapped her legs around my hips.

"Yes."

FOURTEEN

Fiona

From the vantage point of my desk, I watched Halton pace while he spoke on the phone. His long legs covered the distance of his office with ease, and he made the circuit on an endless loop. He tucked his phone between his shoulder and neck, his hands in constant motion, gesturing and waving as his voice rose and lowered during the conversation. He ran a hand through his hair, tugged on his beard, scrubbed his face, sat down, rose again, and paced. He was in constant motion.

I tried not to stare and failed. Dressed in his expensive suit, his hair brushed back from his widow's peak and gleaming under the light, he was sexy, handsome, and irresistible. The draw I felt to him was intense. Undeniable. Unexplainable. Dangerous.

He caught me staring from the desk he had arranged for me in the library, and he winked, laughing in silence as I glanced down, embarrassed at being caught gawking at him.

His voice grew louder as he strode into the library and stopped beside my desk.

"Hold on one second, Phil." He muted his phone.

I glanced up as he leaned down, level with my eyes. "I see you eyeballing me. You like what you see, Fee?"

I could only nod.

He grasped my chin and kissed me. "I like you looking at me."

Then he left. I watched his departure with as much enjoyment as his arrival. He had a great ass. His well-tailored suit showed off all his assets. He looked every inch the successful attorney—cool, calm, and collected—but I knew what was below the finely woven material, the sinewy muscles and strong lines the cloth covered. I knew how he sounded in the heat of passion, the way he felt as he thrust inside me. His warm scent that amplified when he was close enough to touch.

And how I loved to touch him.

Scott had always been distant. Sex had been almost mechanical. Young and inexperienced, I thought it was me. That the whispers and talk of how amazing sex was had just been just that—talk. I had heard some women go on about amazing sex, while others appeared indifferent. Married to Scott, I had accepted indifferent as being my life. Later in our marriage, the absence of sex wasn't an issue. Although I had been truthful when I told Halton it had been four years since Scott and I had been together, it was closer to six years since we'd had anything even somewhat normal. After what I had experienced with Halton, I now knew that sex with Scott was way below normal. On the other hand, sex with Halton was beyond anything I ever could have imagined it to be.

And now, I wasn't sure how I was ever going to go back to indifference or even normal. Halton had woken something inside me that was powerful and addictive.

He was powerful and addictive. I craved him. Constantly.

Rene walked into the library, his hands full of files. "Fee, dear, I need you to sort these and get them prepared for Halton's upcoming meetings."

I took the files and added them to my pile. Halton had a very busy practice. His schedule was full, his hours long, and his dedication clear. He worked hard for his clients. Rene ran a tight office, making sure all Halton had to do was concentrate on his caseload, and I was glad I was able to help him.

"Unacceptable!" Halton snapped, shutting the door between his office and the library. His muted voice still carried, the tone displeased but the words private.

I grimaced. "I wouldn't want to be on the receiving end of that conversation."

Rene chuckled. "No. Once Halton is angry—look out. His clients always benefit."

"No doubt."

Rene tilted his head. "You look well today, my dear. You must have had a good weekend. I'm pleased to see that, considering all that occurred last week."

"Oh," I mumbled. "Yes, it was a relaxing weekend."

I supposed you could call constant sex, long naps, and eating junk food relaxing. I was going to stick to his description.

Rene cast his glance toward Halton's closed door. "Halton looks surprisingly rested. More so than I can remember him looking in a long time. He must have had a good weekend as well." He eyed me with a mischievous grin.

"Ah, I wouldn't know," I replied, but my voice rose toward the end of the statement, and my cheeks felt warm.

Rene's eyes crinkled. "Of course not," he stated. "It's a simple coincidence the two of you both look well today. It does my old heart good."

I picked up the pile of folders. "I had better get at this."

"Right." Rene reached into his pocket. "Halton asked me to make sure you had a copy of this." He handed me a key. "His office. It works on all the doors leading in there." He met my eyes knowingly. "There are three people with keys to his office. Halton, me, and now you."

I accepted the key silently, shocked. I knew what it meant to Halton for him to give me a key to that room. It meant he trusted me —completely.

Rene patted my shoulder kindly. "Be patient with him, dear Fee. He is damaged, but below that veneer of rock is the heart of a man needing to be loved." He lowered his voice. "I've been waiting for this for a very long time. I'm going to enjoy every moment of it."

I didn't know what to say. He winked and left the library.

I sat back, the files momentarily forgotten. Rene didn't

understand. Halton and I were only filling a need for each other. Sleep and sex.

Halton insisted on it. He was very clear when he had set the ground rules and I had agreed to them.

Except...

He was the one to constantly break them. The affection. Spending time together. The kisses. Cuddles. Taking me places. Showing his care and concern.

Still, he was clear on his thoughts about relationships and love. And although his actions said otherwise, he wasn't interested in a lasting relationship. I had to remind myself of that fact.

Rene was wrong. Halton was my lawyer, my friend, and my temporary lover. Nothing more. We were simply filling a void for each other. Once his sleep patterns had adjusted and a new woman caught his eye, my saturation level would be reached, and I would be replaced.

I had to guard my heart. It was already bruised enough.

Halton

Despite how busy the office was and the assholes I dealt with all day Monday, my mood was almost euphoric. I was rested, energized, and in control. A weekend spent gorging on sleep, sex, and Fee had done me a world of good.

I also liked being able to see her whenever I looked up—which I found myself doing often during the day. Usually, her head was bent over some task, her lovely hair shielding her face, but more than once, I had caught her studying me, seemingly unable to look away any more than I could.

I teased her about it, but I also felt the thrill of pride, knowing she liked what she saw. God knew how much I liked looking at her, hearing her voice when she talked to Rene or was on the phone. Her laughter made my lips curl in response, no matter what I was dealing with at the time. My gaze greedily watched her walk toward me, her hair tumbling over her shoulders and down her back in long silver waves. She wore her glasses in the office, which, coupled with her pretty blouses and skirts, gave her a naughty librarian vibe. I had constant fantasies about taking her against the tall oak bookcases in my library while she wore those glasses. Hearing her moan my name in my ear as she came. Feeling her heels dig into my ass as I drove into her. I was determined to make it happen somehow.

Her retreating view was equally spectacular. Her hips swayed as she moved, her A-line skirt showing off her ass to perfection. I knew how that ass looked naked. How plump and supple those cheeks felt under my fingers. How they clenched when I bit them. How perfectly her hips filled my hands as I rode her.

I spent the day with a perpetual hard-on. I constantly adjusted myself, at times closing my door to allow my blood to disperse to other parts of my body for a few moments. The respite was brief since as soon as I saw her again, my cock took notice.

Horny bastard.

Add in the library fantasy, and I was fucked.

And not in a good way.

A knock at my door interrupted my thoughts. With a sigh, I leaned back into the rich leather of my chair.

"In," I called, shutting the file I hadn't really been giving the proper attention.

Reid Matthews strolled in, his usual cocky smile in place. A laptop was tucked under his arm, and his free hand held a cup of coffee. He flung himself into the chair across from me.

"Hey."

"Reid. I wasn't expecting to see you today. I called Wyatt earlier, but all I got was his voice mail."

Reid grinned. "I think you scared him with your attitude last week. Then I showed up at his place, and he was convinced he was out of a great gig. I assured him I was there to help augment the project and his contract was safe."

"Is that a fact?" I asked dryly.

"It is. He does great work. He doesn't like going out into the real world much. So, I'm playing messenger."

There was another knock at my door, and Rene walked in without waiting for a response. He set a hot cup of coffee beside me. "I'll hold your calls. I have Fee busy in the file room."

"Thanks, Rene."

He left, pulling the door shut behind him.

Reid sipped his coffee, grinning over the rim. "So, it's true. Fee is working here?"

I waved my hand. "She had experience in a law office, and Rene needs the assistance."

"Uh-huh." He winked. "I caught a glimpse of her. She rocks that silver hair. Very sexy."

I glared at him, ignoring his remarks, knowing he was trying to goad me. "What did you two come up with?"

He opened the laptop, getting serious. "Wyatt was right. We're not PIs, Hal. I can't tell you about his personal habits. I can only tell you what his computer shows me."

"I know. Wyatt was pissing me off—I needed to light a fire under him."

Reid chuckled. "You did. Wyatt got the message. I can tell you this. Scott is behaving erratically, and I suspect you're right. There are constant withdrawals from his accounts. His billing hours at the law practice are down. Personal bills are overdue. He's taken a second mortgage out on his house." He sucked in a deep breath. "It all started about nine months ago and has been escalating."

"Okay. So, he's using, and his life is falling apart."

"Coincidently, he hired a new assistant around the same time as his behavior became erratic. I checked her out. She isn't good news."

I sat back, rubbing my chin. "Sounds as if she's a bad influence."

"She was up on drug-related charges. And guess who the lawyer was who got her off on those charges?"

I lifted one eyebrow. "Then the stupid fucker hired her?"

"I think so."

I whistled. "How is the company structured?"

"In his favor. He has the final say, the largest shareholder. No one can bring him down." He turned the laptop to face me. "Their financials are good, even with his lack of hours. The firm is solid."

I frowned as I studied the numbers. They were decent, but they seemed wrong somehow. Given the large number of cases they took on, I would have thought their bottom line would have been higher. Personally, Scott was spending a lot of money. There were constant large cash withdrawals. If he had a bad drug habit, it was only going to get worse. He was still comfortable, but if he carried on this way, in a year or so, that would change drastically.

"He threw out an offer on Friday to Fee. Maybe I should tell her to accept."

Reid lifted a shoulder. "We just started digging. Give us a couple more days."

I reached into my drawer and handed Reid the memory stick Fee had given me. "This is information off his private home computer. It has financials on it."

Reid plugged it in, and for a few moments, there was only the sound of the keyboard strokes and his quiet mutterings. He glanced up with a frown.

"Interesting."

"What?"

"There is a completely different set of numbers here. And there is

160

one name that keeps coming up—and I don't remember seeing it in the other books as billable. I did see it noted pro-bono a few times."

I barked out a laugh. "The ass is screwing his partners too? Skimming and hiding it?"

"We need to do some cross-referencing and checking, but I think that, yes, he is."

"What a total bastard."

Reid pushed his hair off his forehead. "I don't think that is big news."

"No. The way he has treated Fee, no. But screwing his partners as well? God knows what other illegal things he has his hands in."

Reid typed fast, studying his screen. "The name is a huge, well-known drug lord. He's constantly in the paper."

"Jesus." I ran a hand over my face. "I need to get Fee out of this and fast."

"Yes." He stood. "Wyatt and I will run with this. You do what you do—"

My personal line rang, interrupting him. I glanced at the screen and held up my finger, hitting the speaker button.

"Smithers."

"Hal, it's Jonas Peters."

"*Scott's guy*," I mouthed to Reid.

"Right. What can I do for you?"

"Scott is willing to make a flat, one-time offer so they can move ahead with the divorce and start fresh."

I snorted. "Your client needs more than a fresh start, Peters. Based on what I saw, he needs a stint in rehab."

There was a pause, then Jonas cleared his throat. "I can't comment on that, Hal. You should advise your client to take the offer. She seems like a nice enough person, and I'd hate to make this ugly. Scott has no issue pushing back. As for the company, you can't get meat from bones, if you catch my drift."

My patience snapped.

"Send an offer, and I'll review it with my client. One million isn't going to cut it. As for the company, I don't care how much bone is showing—I can find all the hidden flesh. And since Fiona isn't in the same rush your client is, we're happy to go to trial, have auditors comb the books, and dig through personal finances for the past ten years. I have an incredibly diligent and thorough investigative team. I bet we'll find a feast fit for a king." I paused. "You can pass that along to your client. Get it to me ASAP—the longer I wait, the more I'm going to fight you."

I hung up.

Reid threw back his head in laughter. "Thank God I'm not on the opposing team."

"Use that drive and find me everything you can. If he plans to fight, he is going to regret it."

He slid the drive into his pocket. "Done."

It was well after six when Fiona came into my office, carrying a stack of folders and a cup of coffee.

"It's decaf," she informed me, setting it beside my elbow.

I grimaced. "It's hot water, then—why bother?"

"Maybe one of the reasons you have trouble sleeping is the fact that you drink coffee constantly. And your fridge is filled with soda— sugary, caffeine-laden soda. You need to cut back, and that might help."

"Your perfect ass pressed against me helps a lot," I retorted. "So does fucking you hard."

Rene froze partway through the door. I met his amused but startled gaze.

"Sorry, I thought you had left," I mumbled.

"I am most certainly leaving now." He spun on his heel, calling over his shoulder. "I'd wish you a good evening, but apparently, you are well ahead of me on that."

I heard the door close, and I dared to look at Fee.

Her eyes were fixed on the carpet, and her fingers worked nervously on the hem of the jacket she had draped around her shoulders.

I drew in a deep breath. "Fee, I'm sorry," I said sincerely. "I thought we were alone. I didn't mean to embarrass you."

Her mouth twitched, once, twice. She leaned back and laughed. Long, melodious peals of laughter. For a moment, I stared, drinking in the sight of her amusement, then I joined her.

"I'm such an ass," I stated.

She wiped her eyes. "Yes. Yes, you are, Halton."

"I'm sorry."

"You're forgiven. Try to rein it in, okay?"

I picked up my coffee and took a sip. It wasn't bad as far as caffeine-free shit went. "Thanks." I lifted my mug in salute of it and her acceptance. Her easygoing nature was amazing to witness. I had never known another woman like her.

"May I talk to you?" Fee asked.

I grimaced. "Of course. You know that." The look on her face made me anxious. "Which hat am I wearing for this conversation?"

"My attorney."

"Ah." Her answer eased some of the tension I felt. What I had been expecting her to say, I wasn't sure, but her attorney, I could handle. I made an over-the-top action of doffing a hat which made her smile. "Ready."

"I've been thinking about Friday."

"And?" I prompted. I had been waiting for this conversation.

"I want to accept Scott's offer and be done with it."

I wasn't surprised, but I had to admit, I was disappointed. I wanted to go after the bastard and make him pay for everything he had done.

"Let's not jump too fast, Fee. In fact, Jonas called earlier, and I told him to send an offer—an official, written one—not something thrown on the table by his client while high."

She looked past me, over my shoulder, her gaze unfocused. "I'm not a vindictive person, Halton."

I snorted. "Yeah, I got that."

She held up her hand. "I grew up simply. My father wasn't wealthy, and when he died, there wasn't anything left for me except enough to pay for the funeral. He didn't even have life insurance. I worked while putting myself, then Scott, through university. I enjoyed working until Scott decided I wasn't good enough to be part of his firm. I volunteered as much as I could since he insisted I wasn't allowed to work anymore. He felt it would reflect badly on him if his wife worked, while none of the other partners' wives did. But I liked to stay busy. Maybe his offer doesn't seem like much to you, but I can get a little place, put the rest aside, and move on with my life. Find a job I enjoy and work there instead of having to work someplace I dislike. I don't plan on sitting around and spending money. That isn't me."

I resisted asking her if she disliked working here—for me. It made sense she would want a clean break once her case was settled. I didn't like it for some reason, but it made sense.

I knitted my fingers together and studied her. "I'm going to be blunt. As Scott's spouse, legally you are entitled to fifty percent of your net worth as a married couple. Including his shares in his company since I plan to get that ridiculous piece of paper struck down. That also means you inherit half of the debt."

She blinked. "Debt? Scott never had any debt. He paid the house off quickly and..." Her voice trailed off as I shook my head.

"Reid was here earlier with some information. Scott took a second mortgage out some months ago. I can argue the house was solely in his name, therefore the debt is his, but we could lose. Reid also found a lot of cash withdrawals from various accounts—even from Scott's retirement fund."

"Is he broke?"

I shook my head. "No. But he is depleting his resources, and it worries me. At some point, there won't be anything left." I didn't say anything about the idea he was skimming from his own company and hiding the money. I would use that when and if needed.

Fee's eyes widened and filled with sadness. "You were right, weren't you? It's drugs."

"I haven't confirmed it yet, but I think so, yes."

She shook her head. "I can't believe he's throwing his life away like that." Her gaze dropped, her voice quiet. "I feel as if I need to reach out to him to try to stop it."

Standing, I crossed to the front of the desk and dropped to my knees in front of her. I gathered her hands in mine, shocked at how cold they were.

"You can't, Fee. You need to stay away from him. You've seen the way the drugs enrage him. I don't want you anywhere near him. Promise me you won't do that."

"Don't I owe him that?"

"No," I stated firmly. "You don't. He's a grown man. He knew the consequences of his choices the second he decided to snort cocaine. He has spent his entire career screwing people over, taking advantage, and being selfish. He relied on the fact that you were so beaten down, you would allow him to dictate this divorce as well. He knows it isn't happening now, so he can fucking well pay the price."

I felt a tremor race through her, so I gentled my voice. "Let's see what the offer is, Fee, and if you want to accept it and move on, I won't force you. You've had enough choices taken away from you already. I won't add to the list. But let me do the job you hired me to do, okay? Let me defend you against him."

She sagged in the chair. "Okay."

"Good. As soon as the offer comes in, we'll talk again."

She nodded and opened her mouth, then closed it.

"What?"

"It's a different hat now."

"All right."

"What is happening, Halton? With us? Is what I'm doing with you any different? Am I not cheating on him?"

"No, you're separated. Your relationship is over—you are both aware of that fact. When he cheated on you, you thought you were still in the relationship together. That's the difference. As for us, Fee...I don't know how to answer that. I like being with you. I enjoy it. Sex with you is incredible..." I hesitated.

"But temporary."

"I told you before I'm not forever—I'm just right now. It's all I have to offer." I tucked a stray lock of hair behind her ear. "One day soon, FeeNellyRaptor, you'll move on to a new life. You'll be the strong, independent woman I know you to be, and you'll find your place." I swallowed down the sudden thickness in my throat. "And you'll find the man who'll love you forever and treat you the way you deserve to be treated. Like the fierce goddess you are."

"And where will you be?" she asked, her voice a whisper in the room.

"Here, doing what I do." I tapped the end of her nose and stood. "I'll be cheering you on, grateful I got to have one sliver of your time, and knowing you made me a better man for it."

She stood and flung her arms around my neck, holding me tight. I gripped her back, feeling the loss of her when she moved away.

She hurried to the door. "Don't work too late, Halton." She paused, her hand on the doorframe. "I'm going to get something to eat and go to the condo. You know where I am later if you want to find me."

We both knew I would.

"Got it."

It hurt to watch her walk away. But I knew it was going to be the same every time she did it, until the day she no longer returned. How I would deal then, I had no idea. But somehow, I would figure it out.

I had no other choice.

I sat down and lost myself in the pile of work in front of me.

That, I knew, would always be there.

FIFTEEN

Halton

An hour later, I glanced at my watch in frustration. I wasn't accomplishing anything. I couldn't concentrate on the files, and I had gone through the same documents time and again. I flipped the folder closed, knowing I had to give up and start again in the morning. I would come in early. I stood and stretched, deciding to grab a bite across the street, then head home.

I walked across the street, pausing by the large windows of my favorite local bar. Sitting at a table was Fee. Her head was down, tilted away, but there was no doubt it was her. The light caught her silver hair cascading down over her shoulders. She was leaning on her elbow, her chin propped up in her hand, staring at the table, her finger tracing an abstract design on the wood. A glass of wine was in front of her, an untouched salad, ignored. I could see the strain of everything in the droop of her shoulders, and the need to somehow ease her worries, fix whatever was weighing on her, hit me.

Something about her made me want to solve everything that was upsetting her. Make her entire world right—even if it was me that was the problem. It was very confusing.

I stared at her for another moment, drinking in her beauty. I lifted my gaze, bristling when I saw a man leaning against the bar, his attention entirely focused on Fee. He sipped his drink, his unwavering gaze piercing. I glared when his eyes met mine, his eyebrows rising and his chin dipping as if to say "look at her," then focused his gaze back on Fee. My hackles rose at the predatory look.

He drained his drink, setting it on the bar, and straightened. He rolled his shoulders as if gearing up for a fight, then turned and began to move toward Fee.

Like a bull seeing a waving cape, I charged forward, my muscles taut and my focus on one thing, and one thing only.

Getting to Fee before that asshole did.

I burst through the door, darting to the right, my legs eating up the distance quickly. I hit the edge of a table, barely stopping long enough to mutter an apology, heading toward Fee and cutting off the jerk. Fee's startled gaze met mine, and before she could say anything, I bent, wrapped my hand around her neck and pulled her in, kissing her hard. She gasped into my mouth but let me pull her close, her mouth moving perfectly with mine.

I eased back. "Hey, love. Sorry I'm late."

She blinked.

"You started without me. Good." I sat down, pulling my chair close. I glanced over my shoulder, meeting the stranger's eyes. He was frozen, one hand clutching the back of a chair as he stared at us. I smirked and lifted my eyebrows. He frowned, and without thinking, I mouthed one word.

"Mine."

He spun on his heel and headed toward the bar.

Fee glanced at me, then toward the bar. "What just happened?"

I turned to her with a grin. "Nothing. I missed you. I thought we could have dinner."

"You missed me," she repeated, the surprise in her voice evident.

"Yep."

"And you knew I'd be here...because?"

I shrugged. "Lucky guess." I looked at her plate. "Tell me that's an appetizer."

"It's my dinner."

"Not anymore." I signaled for the waiter and ordered us cheeseburgers and a basket of fries. I glanced at Fee. "Guinness?"

"No, I'll drink my wine."

I shrugged off my jacket and faced her fully. "Okay."

"What did you do, Halton? Why is that man staring at us?"

I thought of the word I'd mouthed to the jerk-off. What possessed me, I had no idea, but the thought of someone else moving in on Fee made me want to punch something.

"He's probably thinking the same thing I am."

"Which is?"

I grinned and kissed her. "That you're the prettiest woman here. No doubt he's jealous I get to sit beside you and do this." I pulled her in for another long kiss. "Play your cards right, Fee, and I'll let you take me home too."

She laughed softly. "I think you're trying to distract me."

"Is it working?"

"If I say yes, it will encourage your behavior."

"I think you like my behavior."

She rolled her eyes but let me link my fingers with hers. I lifted her hand to my mouth and kissed the tender skin.

I glanced toward the bar, narrowing my eyes at the asshole still staring. He grabbed his coat and walked out of the bar.

"That's right, fucker," I muttered. "Keep walking."

Fee shook her head, understanding dawning across her face. "Incorrigible."

I sat back with a grin and picked up my Guinness. "That's me." I leaned forward. "I think we need to go back to the office after we eat, Fee. There is something in the library I need to do."

"What is that?" she asked.

I narrowed my eyes, my stare intense. My body was fired up with testosterone, and I knew only one way to calm it. My fantasy was going to be played out. Repeatedly.

"You."

By Thursday, my body was teeming with energy. I hadn't been without Fee beside me at night once.

Every morning, I swore I would go it alone that night, and every night, I found my way back to her. It didn't matter if it was on the sofa in her place, her bed, or mine, I slept. As long as she was close, I could relax.

I even felt calmer during the day. In control. Whether it was the sleep, the sex, or Fee, I had no idea.

I was drawn to her. At the office. At home. When I was out at meetings or in court, she was constantly on the shadowy edges of my mind.

Rejuvenated, I worked out harder. My mind was sharper.

And the sex. Never had I experienced the sensations sex with Fee brought me. Unlike past relationships, the more I had sex with Fee, the more I wanted it. At the office—especially the library. Every surface, hard, soft, wall, or counter in the condo. In my car. Every chance I got.

I craved her touch. I could hear her voice and place her in the office, even when my door was closed. Every excuse I could come up with, I found a way to touch her. She was an addiction.

One I wasn't sure how I would live without once this was over.

Because it would be over—it was the way things worked for me.

Fee came into my office, setting some documents on the corner of my desk. "Rene needs you to sign these as soon as possible, please."

I reached for them, my fingers brushing against hers. I tried to keep our time during office hours professional, but I broke my own rule time and again. After the office closed, all bets were off.

And usually, so were our clothes.

"Have I mentioned you look very pretty today?" I inquired. She had her hair down and was wearing a new dress, the deep green emphasizing her eyes.

Her cheeks colored and she smiled. "Thank you. I wanted to look nice for tonight."

"Tonight?"

"I'm having dinner with Joanne."

I frowned. "Did I know about this?"

She shook her head in exasperation. "I mentioned it on the weekend, Halton."

"Where are you going?"

"To The Keg. Not far."

"Take a cab. Call me when you're ready, and I'll pick you up."

She took a stack of files I was done with and held them against her chest, her crossed arms holding them in place. "I will walk there and take a cab back to my place. You don't have to pick me up."

"It'll be dark," I protested, unsure why I felt the need to make sure she was safe.

"I'll be fine, Halton. I'm meeting her at six. I'll be home around nine or so, and I will be fine."

She turned and walked away, her swaying hips teasing me. The dress swung around her knees, the silky fabric grazing the swell of her ass. It was spectacular.

"Then call me when you get there. Both coming and going."

She didn't turn her head, but I knew what her facial expression was without seeing it.

"Stop rolling your eyes at me," I commanded.

Her low laughter confirmed my suspicion.

"Worrywart," she muttered.

"Stubborn woman," I retaliated.

But I was grinning as I dragged the documents closer. I enjoyed sparring with her. More and more of her personality was shining through, and I liked seeing it. My admiration for her grew daily. She endeared herself to me more than I thought possible.

I wasn't certain how I felt about that. But I seemed unable to stop it.

I rubbed my eyes and shut off the desk light. I had worked through everything on my desk and that waited for me on my computer. I was fully caught up—a rare occurrence these days, given how busy my practice had become. I had been mulling over Fee's idea the past few days, thinking she was right. Maybe it was time to bring someone else on board. Another attorney with the same principles as me, who wanted to do some good in this world. Between the two of us, I was certain I could convince Fee to stay on board. There would be enough to keep her and Rene busy. We could even expand the office and add a third body to help out.

I walked to my car, still thinking. I glanced at my watch, wondering if Fee was home now. I already knew I would seek her out. I had given up the fight, deciding to enjoy the peace she gave me and the sleep I was getting used to while I could.

It was past ten, dark, and the streets quieter than usual as I steered my car out of the garage and headed toward the condo. I turned down the street where my building was located, intent on getting home, having a shower, and going to Fee. Her bed was smaller, but I preferred knowing she was safe at home when I returned to my condo in the early hours of the morning and got ready for work. She still insisted on separate vehicles, and I had stopped fighting her.

I was still waiting for Scott's offer. Jonas had requested an extension, and I had the feeling he was having trouble pinning Scott down. The delay worked in our favor, but I was looking forward to putting the screws to them as soon as possible.

As I sat at a red light, I glanced to my left when the flash of something bright under the streetlight caught my eye.

I froze when I realized what I was seeing. Fee was standing on the sidewalk, arguing with someone.

Scott.

As I watched, he gripped her shoulders, pushing her back against the brick of the building beside her, shaking her fast.

Rage tore through me, clouding my brain. I didn't wait for the light to change. Not giving a shit for my own safety, I hit the gas, tearing through the red light. The car screeched to an abrupt stop, and I slammed it into park and flung open the door so fast, the hinges creaked in protest. I ignored the honks of other cars that had to veer around mine I had left abandoned. My entire concentration was on Fee and the asshole who had her pinned. I could hear her voice pleading with him to calm down and let her go as my feet pounded against the cement. A noise escaped my throat—one I was certain I had never made until that moment—a low, almost feral growl.

Fee's terrified gaze met mine, her eyes widening in relief and alarm as she saw the murderous look on my face. I sank my hands into Scott's shoulders, pressing hard, and tore him away from Fee, sending him sprawling to the sidewalk. I stepped in front of Fee, protecting her with my body as I glared down at him.

"Are you okay?" I asked, turning my head. "Did he hurt you?"

"He-he scared me," she replied, her voice shaking. "But I'm okay."

I found her hand in the dark and squeezed it, then focused my attention on the man struggling to get to his feet. "What the hell are you doing, Scott?" I demanded.

He glared up at me, his eyes unfocused and dark. The bastard was high again.

"Talking to my wife. Leave us alone," he spat at me, his body twitching.

"I will say this one more time. She isn't your wife anymore. You kicked her out, and you've lost the right to call her that." I shook my head. "Where is your common sense? You have screwed your entire case with this bonehead move. Attacking my client with witnesses?" I laughed, the sound dry and rough. "You can kiss your case goodbye, Scott. I am going to make it my number one priority to see you pay for this stunt."

He made a strange face, trying to appear tough. "Fuck off, Smithers. I want to talk to Fiona."

"You talk to her through me. With your attorney present." I narrowed my eyes. "Walk away, Scott. I'll call the police if you don't."

He shifted his weight from one foot to the other, trying to find his center of gravity. He pursed his lips.

"You fucking her?"

I dropped Fee's hand and stepped forward. My voice was menacing to my own ears as I spoke.

"Last chance, Scott. Stop disrespecting Fee and walk away. You're already in enough trouble."

He snarled and began to step back. I saw his hand curling into a fist, and I was ready, knowing what he was about to do and welcoming the chance. As he lifted his arm, ready to strike, I knocked away his ineffectual punch and hit him with a punch of my own. It caught him fully in the nose, sending him sprawling back to the cement, blood spurting down his face.

He screamed like a little girl, holding his face.

"I'm suing you for assault," he yelled.

"Go ahead." I looked at the small crowd that had gathered. "Anyone see me attack him first?"

A woman stepped forward. "I'll be a witness. I saw him attack this woman and then attack you when you came to her defense. You got here before I could," she added.

A couple of other people nodded, and I looked down at Scott. "I think you better call Jonas," I informed him. "Your problems just got worse."

I slid my hand into my pocket, ignoring the dull ache in my knuckles, and handed the people who had agreed to be witnesses my card. I took their information on my phone, never moving from in front of Fee or taking my eyes off Scott for long. He sat up, his head lowered, holding his sleeve to his nose.

When I was done, I dragged Scott to his feet. He glared at me as I snapped a photo.

"You're going to regret this, Smithers," he vowed. "I'm going to end you."

I laughed at his empty threat. "Get out of my sight, Scott, before I do something I might regret. Like you're going to regret this in the morning."

With a final glare, he uttered one last warning. "This isn't over," he snarled at Fee.

I stepped in front of him, blocking his view. "It is," I spat. "You did this, and now you're going to pay for it."

He wiped his nose. "She isn't worth it."

"That's where you're wrong, Scott. One day you'll crawl out of the hole you've dug for yourself and realize how worth it she is—but it will be too late. Now, get out of here. It's the last time I'll say it."

He stumbled away, disappearing around the corner.

I turned back to Fee, taking in her shaking form and the shock written across her face.

Wrapping an arm around her waist, I pulled her close. "It's okay, Fee. I have you. I'll take you home now, okay?"

"Don't-don't leave me."

I tucked her closer.

"I promise."

SIXTEEN

Halton

I led Fee to my car, buckling her in when her shaking hands refused to cooperate. I drove the short distance home and kept her tucked to my side until we reached my condo. I led her to the bathroom and slid my fingers under her chin, forcing her to meet my eyes. She hadn't said a word to me since I got her in the car, although she had held my hand with a death grip the entire time.

"I need to check you over, okay?"

She looked at her arms. "He tore my dress," she whispered, touching the frayed fabric at her shoulder. "I just bought it."

"I'll replace it."

She let out a long, shuddering breath. "He came out of nowhere. I was almost home, and suddenly he was there, yelling at me."

"Why were you walking, Fee? I told you to take a cab home."

"Joanne and I shared a cab. She was headed to Union for the train, and I had the cab drop me at the corner. It was only a couple of blocks to walk. I had no idea..." Her voice trailed off. "He appeared out of nowhere and starting screaming."

I tamped down my anger and slid the zipper down from the base of her neck. She didn't move as I tugged her dress off her shoulders, hissing in anger at the marks on her arms. Bruises were already forming from the grip he'd had on her.

I turned her to face the mirror, showing her the marks. "Fee—he fucking assaulted you. Again. This needs to go on the record. He should be charged. I'm calling the police."

She dropped her eyes, worrying her lip. I turned her back to me and took some pictures of the marks. "Let me do what I need to do."

"Halton, please." She swallowed. "What if he sues you for punching him? It would be bad for you."

I stared at her in disbelief. She was more worried about me than herself. About my reputation. Typical Fee. Sweet, wonderful Fee.

"I can take care of myself. Stand up to him, Fee. Don't let him get away with treating you like this anymore."

For a moment, fear held her still. Then she straightened her shoulders. "You're right."

"Good girl." I brushed a kiss to her forehead. "I'll handle this." I leaned over and pushed the plug down in the tub and turned on the taps. "You're going to have a bath and try to relax. I'm going to make some calls."

"You'll be close?" she asked, her voice anxious.

"I'll be right outside the door."

"Okay."

I called Rene and told him what had occurred. Then I called Aiden, asking for advice. He gave me the name of a cop he was friends with to contact and suggested I have someone around to protect Fee and myself.

"If he's strung out on drugs and acting erratically, you might want to consider protection. You never know what he might do next if he feels cornered."

"You have someone in mind?"

"Yep. I'll send them over tomorrow."

I agreed and thanked him, grateful for the friendship I had with the BAM boys and their connections.

Then I texted Jonas, informing him of what occurred. His response was swift and filled with apologies and pleas not to include the police. He promised to keep Scott away from Fee and assured me he would push the divorce through as fast as possible. I texted him back the picture of Fee's bruises and the one of Scott I had taken. With the dried blood around his nose and the wild, dark glare at the camera, it showed exactly what it should—an out-of-control, drugged-up, desperate man.

Jonas didn't respond. I didn't expect him to.

My last call was to the cop. I got his voice mail and left a message. Scott had already been given too many passes. It ended here.

Then I went to check on Fee.

She was in the tub, her arms wrapped around her legs, her head resting on her knees. Her shoulders shook, and I knew she was crying.

Something happened to me when I saw her cry. I had witnessed countless tears in my life. From clients, witnesses, the women I dated, even Rene on occasion, but they never affected me in any way. Fee's tears, however, did something to me—caused a reaction, a need to comfort and care. To solve whatever was causing her pain and ease it.

Without a word, I shed my clothes and slid in behind her, drawing her close to my chest and wrapping my arms around her.

"Careful," I instructed gently and turned on the tap to add some hot water to the bath which had grown tepid. I moved my legs, distributing the heat, then shut off the water.

Fee leaned into me, her body tight and anxious.

I rubbed her shoulders, wanting to loosen the muscles.

"Let it out, love."

She turned her face, resting her cheek against my chest and wept openly. I held her, cupping water and pouring it onto her skin to keep her warm, mumbling quiet assurances that she was fine. I was here. Everything would be okay.

Finally, her sobs stopped.

"I was so scared," she admitted, her voice rough.

"So was I."

"Why?"

I tightened my hold on her. "I saw him grab you. All I could think of was getting to you before he hurt you." I drifted my fingers over her arms. "I was too late."

She lifted her head, her beautiful eyes red-rimmed and tired. "No, you saved me, Halton."

I ran my finger over her pale cheek. "You're staying here, with me, until this is done. We'll get your things in the morning."

She opened her mouth, and I held a finger to her lips to stop her disagreement. "No arguing. I'm driving you to work and home. I'm not going to risk you again. I might not be around to stop him next time. He's irrational and erratic. I can't risk it. Don't ask me to."

Her breathy sigh was warm against my skin. "Okay."

"And I have security coming as an added precaution."

"You think that's necessary?"

"Yes."

"Okay." She agreed again without argument.

I pulled her back, letting her relax against my chest. I rested my chin on her head, holding her tight. I couldn't find the words to express the fear I had felt when I saw Scott with her earlier. The rage that overcame me when I knew he was hurting her. The desire to rip him apart limb from limb with my bare hands for even approaching her. I couldn't tell her, because I didn't understand it. The emotions I felt with Fee were all new, at times frightening, and definitely overwhelming.

I didn't want to talk about things I didn't understand.

Instead, I held her until the water cooled, then carried her to my bed and lost myself in her, taking my time and drawing out her climax slowly.

I braced myself over her, watching as the ecstasy flitted across her face, our eyes locked, the intense emotion of the moment binding us together. Pleasure rippled down my spine as I orgasmed. I entwined our hands, our fingers clutched tightly as her name escaped my lips. I lowered my head to her neck, kissing the damp skin as my body shuddered and shook, the aftereffects of my orgasm strong.

I slid my arms around her, gathering her close. For a moment, there was silence. Our chests moved in unison, one breathing in while the other breathed out, our skin always touching.

"We just made love," she murmured. "At least, that's what it felt like to me."

I kissed her brow, knowing she was right. It felt that way to me as well. To my body anyway. My heart remained intact.

My chest ached because I knew this would end soon.

I didn't do love. I didn't do relationships. I didn't know how. I didn't have the capacity.

And I was certain I would fail, even if I tried.

For the next few days, I dealt with the aftermath of Scott's attack on Fee. The police, his attorney, the security Aiden had sent over. Fee showed her strength once again, giving her statement in a quiet but steady voice. I added in my account, and the police followed up with the witnesses I had given them the information for.

Then I left it up to them to carry forth justice.

My phone rang late in the afternoon on Monday, and I frowned looking at the number.

"Smithers."

"Jonas Peters here."

"What can I do for you?"

"There has been a development with Scott."

"The development had better be the fucking proposal I've been waiting for and an apology with the assurance he will never to come close to Fee again."

"He's gone into rehab."

I tossed my pen on the desk and rubbed my eyes.

"Are you serious?"

"Yes. His partners convinced him it was in the best interest of everyone involved."

"In his best interest," I snapped. "Great way to avoid the fallout."

"He admitted to his drug addiction, Hal. He wants to move past this and get help." He paused. "His, ah, assistant, was let go from the firm as well."

I snorted. "His assistant, girlfriend, and supplier you mean?"

There was silence. Then he spoke.

"I have a settlement proposal I'm sending to you tomorrow. I think you'll find it fair."

"I'll let you know when I see it."

I hung up.

That fucking bastard. I would bet my last dollar rehab was simply a stunt to buy him some time, escape jail, and maybe garner Fee's sympathy. He wasn't fucking getting mine.

I picked up my pen, tapping it impatiently on the desk. I decided to wait and see the proposal before discussing this with Fee. I wanted to see the offer before I told her.

I waited until the office closed the next day and we were alone. Rene still came in part time, but he was putting in more hours than I wanted him to. He insisted he was bored at home, and with Fee in the office, he enjoyed being there. I had to admit he was right. The office was a great place, and I thought we made a good team. Still, I liked the times when it was only Fee and me.

But for now, I had to wear my attorney hat. I handed her the offer and explained the terms.

"It's a flat settlement. He is offering two million, Fee. He'll release you from any of his debts. He's going to sell the house. But that's it. You have to agree not to go after the business and that we will stop any other inquiries."

"That's a lot of money, Halton."

"It is." I sighed. "I think he's hiding money somewhere, Fee. Stealing from his own firm. Reid suspects we've only scratched the surface. We could push this."

She passed a hand over her eyes, staring into space for a moment in thought.

"At what cost?" she asked quietly. "Me worrying he is going to show up and do something? You overprotective and tense all the time? A security person standing outside the door all day and night?"

She held up her hand before I could speak. "He's in rehab, supposedly to get his life back on track. I hope he does. I hope he moves on. I want to move on. What he has done or not done to his partners is between him and them. I don't care—I just want this done. I think we've punished each other enough."

"How do you think you punished him, Fee?"

She shrugged. "I think maybe I failed him by not being as strong as I should have been. As strong as the person I thought I was years ago. I let him push me around. I allowed him to belittle me and make me into the weak woman I became. He failed me...well, in many ways. But it's in the past. I don't want to be filled with bitterness and resentment anymore." She huffed out a long breath. "It's all in the past, Halton, and I want it to stay there. Accept the offer please and get me my divorce. Let me move forward with my life—whatever direction that is."

I disagreed vehemently with her assessment. I opened my mouth, but she shook her head.

"I know you want to go after him and the business. Dig around and find out if he's hiding money. But it's my decision. I need closure, and you are the person who can get it for me."

I had no choice. She was the client, and the decision was hers. I could advise, suggest, and offer my opinion, but the final word was hers.

"I'll get in touch tomorrow. He's paying all the legal bills, and I'm adding in a no-contact clause. I don't want him near you. He breaks that, we go after him."

"Thank you." She hesitated. "If Scott is in rehab, can you call off the security?"

I knew she hated the extra security. "Already done."

She stood. "Okay."

I watched her go back to her desk and sit. She lowered her head, picking up a pen and going back to work. I thought of the ways I wanted to nail Scott. Reid had sent me information, along with the drive, showing without a doubt Scott was skimming extra money from his firm. He was screwing everyone in his life without regard for anyone but himself. At some point, it was all going to catch up with him.

I rubbed the back of my neck. I would make sure she got her money and was settled. If by chance, one of his partners received a package containing information about a different set of books, it wouldn't be any skin off my nose. Scott in a dispute with his own firm would be entertaining to witness from afar.

I stored the idea away. Fee would hate me for it, and I'd have to be careful not to let it lead back to me.

The next day, I sent Fee to grab some lunch. With Scott in rehab, I figured she was safe going across the street, but I stood, watching her as she disappeared into the building. I told Rene my idea, and he stared at me, his mouth agape.

"No, Halton. Leave it be."

"He deserves to lose everything."

"I agree. But you need to step back. Stop looking at this from a personal point of view."

"I beg your pardon?"

He crossed his good arm over his chest. "When Wanda Dutton hired you for her divorce, you found out some terrible information on her husband that could destroy him but had nothing to do with her situation. You did exactly what you were supposed to do. You got her the divorce she wanted and walked away. This is the same situation. You are reacting from emotion, not logic. Leave it be."

I shook my head. "He made it personal, coming after Fee."

"Tammy Water's husband came after her. You made sure he went to jail for it. You didn't set out to personally destroy him. Step back, Halton. Don't risk your career over someone who isn't worth it." He narrowed his eyes. "You aren't thinking clearly."

I opened my mouth to argue with him, then snapped it shut.

He was right.

"Fuck," I swore. His words struck home.

"Give me that memory drive."

"Why?"

"To stop temptation. Do your job, Halton. Get Fee her freedom, and let the rest of it go."

I slapped the drive into his hand with more force than was necessary. "I might need it."

Rene slid it into his pocket. "It will be in a safe place. You tell me what it is needed for, and I will give it to you."

He paused at the door, looking back at me. "I never thought I would see this day, Halton."

"What day?" I snapped, flinging myself into my chair.

He laughed, his head falling back in amusement.

"That's the best part—you have no clue."

"Stop talking in riddles, old man. Spit it out."

"Nope. I am enjoying this way too much."

"Get out of my office."

His laughter haunted me the rest of the day.

Fee was quiet all evening—contemplative. Her phone had rung a couple of times, then fell silent.

"Anything wrong?" I asked.

She shook her head with a grin. "No. Joanne is in town at a show, and she had an extra ticket. She wanted me to join her."

"You should go," I encouraged her, thinking it would help distract her. "I can drop you off. Is it a play?"

Her mouth curled into a grin. "Um, not exactly."

"A concert?"

"Some might call it that. More of a revue."

I scratched my head. "A revue?"

She laughed quietly. "Think the *Men of Chippendales*."

I widened my eyes in shock. "Oh, ah, I see."

"I said no." She picked up her tablet. "I'm not interested."

I glanced back at my document, the words no longer holding my interest. I looked back up, curious.

"Why not? I thought women liked those shows."

She lifted one shoulder. "Some women."

I frowned. "Not you?"

She peeked up, grinning impishly. "Why would I want to go ogle some strange man's abs when I have perfection in front of me?"

I sat up a little straighter. "Perfection?"

She snorted, the sound making me chuckle. "Give it up, counselor. You know you have a rocking hot body."

I shot her a leer. "A guy likes to hear it sometimes."

"You do. If you were performing, I'd go see you. Instead I'll sit here and imagine it."

"How would I perform?" I asked, my interest piqued.

She huffed out a breath. "Bare-chested, maybe a tie, and your briefcase. That hat I saw in your closet. Black boxers."

I raised one eyebrow. "No pants?"

"Not for long."

I chuckled. "Okay, then."

"You would strut around flexing your muscles and doing that thrust-y thing."

I was enjoying this. "Thrust-y thing?"

"You know." She bent two fingers and waved them up and down. "With your hips."

"Right."

"You'd be a hit."

"I'll keep it in mind in case the attorney thing doesn't work out."

She giggled, once again looking down at her tablet. "Good plan."

Fiona

My book wasn't holding my attention, but Halton was still working on one of his files. He had gotten up a few moments ago to get a book from his office. I stretched my arms over my head, wondering how much longer he would be. I was hoping not long so I could tempt him into going to bed early. The talk about him stripping had cemented in my head, and now all I could think about was him naked and thrusting into me.

Hard.

With Halton, I had discovered a part of me I didn't know existed. He brought out the sensual side I had denied for so many years. Sex with Scott had been tepid at best. Sex with Halton was mind-blowing. Thrilling. Addictive. He pleasured me in ways I didn't realize could happen, and I found myself reciprocating, wanting to give him some of the ecstasy he so freely brought out in me. He made me feel sexy. Beautiful. Wanton and needy.

I sighed and turned off my tablet. I was about to get up when music began to play from the speakers. A low, sensuous beat filled the room. I gaped when Halton appeared in the doorway.

He held his hat dipped low over his eyes and wore only a bright blue tie and boxers. His briefcase was in front of him, and he posed in the doorway, his pecs tight, arms bulging, and abs crunched in a perfect six-pack. He raised his head, his lips curled into a devilish grin.

"Welcome to the show, FeeNelly."

Then he began to move. Slow, sexy steps that brought him closer. He stopped in front of me and doffed his hat, placing it on my head. He bent and kissed me. "Private, for your eyes only, love."

I giggled and lifted my arms in appreciation.

What a show.

His briefcase was discarded, revealing a far more stimulating offering. His cock was erect, straining against the black cotton. He moved to the beat of the music, bending, stretching, arching, and yes—thrusting. He shimmied and shook, stopping to drop kisses to my lips and letting me stroke him.

I wished I had a bunch of bills to stuff into his waistband. Instead, I clapped and whistled, slapping his ass when he turned and bent, the offering too good to resist. He turned, his eyes dark. "Touching the merchandise, Fee?"

My breath caught as he pulled his tie over his head and dropped it around my neck, tightening it so it rested on my collarbone. "I like my clothes on you."

I looked down, blushing. I had grabbed the T-shirt he had discarded earlier and worn it after dinner. It smelled like him and was so long, it brushed low on my thighs.

He bent and laid his hands on my knees, pressing his thumbs into the dimples and then pulling my legs apart. He eased closer, his crotch at eye level as he gyrated, moving his hips in time to the beat of the music. He ran his hands over his torso, lifting his arms in the air and thrusting his pelvis.

"You want to touch, baby?"

I nodded, my throat too dry to speak.

He flexed his pecs, making me whimper.

"Are you wet for me, Fee?"

"Yes."

"You like what you see?"

"Uh-huh."

"Show me how much you like it. Spread those legs wide for me."

I did as he instructed, shimmying forward and pulling up the T-shirt. He traced the edges of my lacy underwear.

"You are wet," he moaned. "Fuck, I love that."

He wrapped his hand around the tie and tugged me closer. "You know what else I love, Fee? Rewards. Rewards for a job well done," he murmured.

"I have no money." I played along, knowing exactly what he wanted.

He yanked on the tie, and I slid my hands around his waist, dropping them to his tight ass and squeezing.

"You have something I want much more," he rumbled, stepping closer so his cock grazed my mouth.

I yanked down his boxers, his erection springing free. I wrapped my hand around it and stroked the velvet steel. "Then let me reward you."

Seconds later, I had his hot, heavy cock in my mouth. He groaned as I glided my tongue along the underside, teasing the crown, then took in as much of him as I could. He slipped his hands into my hair, not pulling or yanking, but guiding and light.

"Oh fuck, Fee. *Yes*. Like that."

I gripped his ass tighter, slumping down farther into the sofa.

He fell forward, resting his hands on the back of the sofa. I arched closer, never releasing his cock from my mouth.

"Don't stop, Fee. Don't you dare stop," he grunted.

I loved his reactions. The way I could make him fall apart. I sucked and licked. Teased and stroked. Moved one hand from his ass so I could play with his balls. He cursed and praised. Begged me to stop. Pleaded with me not to. I dug my fingers into the hard curves of his ass and swallowed.

He flung his head back, shouting my name as he came down my throat, the hot liquid filling my mouth. I took all he gave me, moaning around him and digging my nails into his firm ass.

When he was done, he stepped back, his semi-hard cock slipping from my lips. He gazed down at me, his chest heaving, his cheeks flushed from exertion.

"That was some reward."

"That was some dance."

"Was the thrust-y thing good?" He grinned.

"Meh, I think so."

He bent, lifting me into his arms. I wrapped my legs around his waist, gasping as he carried me to the closest wall. The cold, smooth surface hit my back, his erection already growing between my legs. I rubbed my wet center against him.

"Let's see if I thrust-y better when I'm balls deep inside you."

I held on for dear life.

This was going to be an even better dance. I knew it.

I was looking forward to feeling the rest of his moves.

SEVENTEEN

Halton

I stared at the documents in front of me, drumming my fingers on the desk as I went over them. Seeing the settlement for Fee typed out, the documents signed, and the offer in black and white disturbed me somehow.

I wasn't sure if it was due to the fact that it wasn't the amount I had wanted to get for her, the fact that Scott had followed through and signed the papers, or what it meant, knowing her divorce would move ahead and she would be free to live her life how she wanted.

With whomever she wanted.

The implications of which pressed at the corners of my mind.

Rene walked in, setting a cup of coffee on my desk. "What's with the face?"

I reached for the coffee, glancing around Rene. Fee was still out, her desk chair empty.

"Fee's divorce papers."

He sat. "Ah. Not good?"

"It's fine. Two million. She assumes none of his debt but claims nothing against the business." I snorted. "And a nondisclosure about their marriage, the settlement, and everything surrounding it."

He nodded slowly. "Given what you found out, it's not a bad offer."

I scrubbed my face. "No, it's decent. Given his behavior, the drug issues, and the fact that his partners are at war with him over his drug use, I'm not surprised Jonas added a non-disclosure. Not that Fee would ever discuss any of this with people. She's too private a person."

"Why do you look so pissed off?"

"I wanted to get her more. I could push and get her twice this, if she allowed me to. I could bankrupt them all."

"At what cost?" he asked, sounding so much like Fee that my lips quirked. "She doesn't want blood, Halton. She wants to be free. This settlement can do that for her." He cocked his head. "I've said this before. Don't make this about you or your pride, or even what *you* want for her. Fee wants it done. Let the decision be hers."

He was right. I flipped over the documents. "Okay. I'll go through them with her when she returns."

"What will happen next?"

I frowned in confusion. Rene knew as well as I did the next steps in divorce proceedings. He rolled his eyes at my expression.

"Not legally, Halton. With Fee."

"As you pointed out, her choice."

"Does she have a job here?"

"If she wants it. I thought you liked her."

"Very much. She's a hard worker and makes things easier around here for me."

"Then she stays."

"And your personal relationship?"

That was a far tougher question to answer, and I knew I had to proceed carefully.

"I'm something—someone—she needs right now, Rene. Once her life settles, she'll find the person she is meant to be with."

He arched his eyebrow at me. "Who is to say she hasn't already found him?"

I shook my head. "She knows my limitations. I was clear with her. We're both on the same page. I won't hurt her, Rene. Once she lands on her feet, she'll walk away and find her life."

He stood, staring at me, perplexed.

"When will you find yours, Halton?"

I waved my hand, indicating my office. "*This* is my life, Rene. That hasn't changed."

"No?"

"No, it hasn't."

He shook his head and headed toward the door. "For an incredibly smart man, you are extremely dense at times, Halton."

I glared at his retreating figure but didn't comment. We had two very different views on this subject. Rene saw what he wanted, what he hoped to see.

My view was based on one thing—reality. He simply didn't want to accept it.

Fee looked over the papers, studying the areas I had marked. A curl escaped her hair clip, falling over her face, and she pushed it back, sighing when it fell back over her forehead. I thought of last night. My impromptu dance to make her smile and forget all the shit swirling in her head.

I smiled as I remembered the epic blow job and wild wall sex that followed. As always happened with Fee, I got carried away. She brought out the caveman in me, whether it was seeing another man look at her, me touching her body, or simply the thought of her walking away.

I tried not to think of what the papers she was holding meant for us.

She set down the papers and held out her hand. "I need a pen."

"Are you certain, Fee? We can push back. There's nothing else you want?"

She paused. "I need to return to the house and get a few boxes from the basement."

"I can arrange that. Nothing else?"

"No." She met my gaze with a sad look. "Let it be done, Halton. I need it to be over."

I handed her my pen. "Okay, Fee."

Two weeks went by, and nothing changed. Nothing. The apartment I rented for her sat empty and unused, and I didn't care. Fee was still at my place, sleeping beside me every night, at my side during the day. I knew things would change soon enough, but I hadn't yet brought up the subject. When she had hesitantly suggested leaving, I informed her I would prefer to watch over her until the papers were complete and Scott was removed from her life totally.

She hadn't argued.

I refused to delve into my insistence at her staying with me and what it meant. I was simply being cautious, I told myself.

I ignored the laughter in my head that followed that thought.

Late Tuesday afternoon, Jonas reached out to let me know that Scott had signed himself out of rehab.

"A little soon for that, isn't it?" I asked, feeling anxious at the thought of him out and free to "bump into" Fee.

"He signed himself in freely, so he could leave anytime," Jonas stated mildly. "He insists he's fine. Scott knows what he needs to do to stay clean."

"I hope he stays that way."

"The papers have been signed. I will courier them over tomorrow, along with Fee's settlement. Since neither side is arguing, the divorce should happen quickly."

"Good. I'll let my client know. I'll send my bill to you. I'll have Rene prepare it."

"Fine." He paused. "She got her things?"

Jonas had arranged for Fee to have access to the house. I accompanied her, and a lawyer from Jonas's firm had been present. Fee took six boxes that had her name on them from the basement, which I carried out to the car. I found her in the dining room, holding a small vase, the crystal dull in the light, dusty from neglect.

"Do you want that?" I asked.

She sighed. "Scott gave me this on our first anniversary. I had seen it in a window of a little secondhand shop, and I thought it was beautiful. He filled it with flowers and promised me he would always keep it full." She traced the rim with her finger, looking sad.

"Another promise broken," I muttered.

She stared down at the vase. "It's hard to reconcile the man who swore to love me and never forgot to bring home a bunch of flowers every week with the man I know now. Sometimes I wonder if he ever remembers that I was once important to him."

I had no response for her.

"Is it silly to want this—to want to remember a time when he wasn't the man he is today?" she asked, her voice shaking with emotion.

I hated the thought of her having anything from him, but I knew that was my own resentment talking. For some reason, when it came to her, I felt incredibly possessive, even though I didn't have that right.

"No, Fee. It might be nice for you to keep a good memory. You can

take it. I'll add it to the list I'm sending his attorney," I advised. "Anything else?"

She looked around and shook her head.

Looking around the cold, austere house, it didn't surprise me. I saw none of Fee's warmth in the place. It was decorated to impress and didn't feel like a home. I was glad when she announced she wanted to leave.

"Yes. She doesn't need to go back."

"The house is going up for sale next week."

I didn't really care, but I made an appropriate remark back to Jonas. He said goodbye and hung up. I sat looking at the phone, wondering how this would affect Fee. Affect us.

I had my answer the next day.

Fee stared at the draft, holding the narrow paper in her hand.

"This is a lot of money. Is it customary for a person to get the settlement before the divorce is final?"

I shrugged. "Depends on the case. Scott wanted it this way. I wasn't going to argue since I wanted you to have the money as soon as possible."

"Have you been paid?"

I grinned. "Rene sent my bill."

"Should I pay you as well?"

"No, that is part of the agreement. Scott pays the legal fees. He did this, so he is paying. It's all good, Fee."

"All right." She looked back at the draft, still unsure.

"I can recommend a financial person. A woman, actually. I use her. So does Rene. She can advise you regarding taxes and investments."

She met my eyes. "I've been looking at houses online."

Something strange happened in my chest. It pinched and burned, tightening and making me uncomfortable. I picked up a glass of water and drained it, hoping the feeling would go away.

"A house?" I repeated.

She nodded, looking past me to the window and the skyline.

"Obviously, I need a place, and I don't think I'm a condo person." She looked at me. "Not that I haven't appreciated your hospitality. But I know you want your space back. I'm sure I've imposed long enough."

My hospitality.

Why did those words rankle so badly?

I cleared my throat, unsure how to reply. Fee had never "imposed," as she called it. I couldn't recall thinking I wanted her to leave, although I knew eventually it would happen.

She was correct, of course. Now was the time.

The odd sensation in my chest rose again, and I rubbed at my sternum. I must have eaten something that disagreed with me. That had to be it.

"Where are you looking?" I finally spoke, my voice sounding rough.

"Around the Islington area. Close for commuting, but there are some lovely little spots."

I could only nod.

She stood. "I guess I had best take this to the bank and deposit it."

"Good plan."

"I might go and see a few places this weekend. Did you...did you want to come?"

"I promised Carl I would give them some extra time on Saturday. I've been a bit neglectful as of late. Sorry," I lied.

She looked disappointed but not surprised.

"Sure, I understand."

She walked back to the library, for the first time shutting the door between us.

I stared at the wood that separated us. Somehow, I knew it was the beginning of our end.

The pain in my chest spasmed once again.

This time, I ignored it.

Rene rapped on my door, his face anxious as he poked his head around the frame.

"Halton, Jonas is on line one."

I frowned at his voice and wondered why Jonas hadn't called my private line as usual. I picked up the receiver. "Jonas."

A few moments later, I hung up, staring into space. Rene came in, his expression mirroring my own. He already knew.

"Where is Fee?"

"Out getting lunch."

I rubbed a hand across my face. "We're going to need some privacy."

"I rescheduled your one p.m. to three."

"Okay."

"Where does this leave her?" he asked.

I shrugged as I heard the outer door open. "That's what remains to be seen."

Fee came in, carrying a bag. Things had been off between us the past few days. She had been quiet at night, often slipping off to bed early. During the day, she was more withdrawn than before, and I knew our impending goodbye was weighing heavily on us.

The only time things seemed normal was in the dark of the night when I would slide in beside her and take her into my arms. The sex was quieter yet still intense, and the aftermath was profound. I held her tightly, seeking the solace of her embrace, needing it to sleep and wishing I could express the rampant thoughts in my head. Wanting to ask her to talk to me.

But we remained silent.

I watched her approach my desk, wondering how she would handle the news I had to share. What her reaction would be.

She frowned as she took in my expression and set down the bag she was carrying.

"Halton? What is it?"

I stood and took her hand, leading her to the sofa. Rene discreetly shut my door, giving us privacy.

"I have some news, Fee."

"All right?"

I gathered both her hands in mine. "It's Scott."

"What has he done?" she whispered.

I tightened my grip. "He's dead, Fee."

She stared at me, shocked and disbelieving.

"What?"

"There was an accident."

"Did-did this have something to do with drugs?" she asked, her fingers gripping the edge of my jacket.

"No." I knew I had to tell her the truth. "He was high, though. He stumbled out onto the road and was hit by a truck. He died before he got to the hospital."

She shook her head in sorrow. "He was using again." Tears glimmered in her eyes. "What a waste of his life." She gripped my jacket tighter. "I know you knew him as a jerk, but Halton, at one time, he was a decent guy. He wanted to make a difference." A tear slid down her face. "He got lost."

I rubbed her hands, which had turned cold. "I know, Fee. If you loved him once, he must have been a good guy."

"What-what happens now?"

"You're still listed as next of kin on all his documents. I guess he hadn't gotten around to changing that. Do you know what he wanted?"

She nodded in silence, her eyes wide and shocked.

"I don't know what to do," she whispered.

"Rene and I will help, Fee. You aren't alone. Jonas will assist as well." He had been decent on the phone, obviously as shocked as Fee over Scott's death.

"Okay," she murmured. "But I need a few moments."

I stood and pressed a kiss to her forehead. "Of course."

I wrapped a blanket around Fee's shoulders, noticing the coffee I had given her hadn't been touched.

In the days since Scott's death, she had been withdrawn and quiet, which wasn't a surprise. Scott's girlfriend had been so vehement and vocal with her grief that Fee stepped back and allowed her to handle the arrangements. Fee didn't attend the service, instead choosing a brief, private visit to the funeral home. I waited outside for her, and when she returned to the car, she was calm and at peace.

The peace only lasted a couple of days, when Scott's girlfriend had discovered Fee was also still listed as the beneficiary of all Scott's worldly goods, including a large life insurance policy he had. She had shown up at the office unannounced, high, screaming and yelling about Fee stealing her rightful inheritance. She ranted about suing Fee and taking her to court, and how she was the woman in Scott's life, not Fee, and Fee was stealing her money. Security had removed her, but the damage was done.

Fee had shut down.

I glanced at Rene, who was sitting next to Fee, holding her hand. He had been a rock for her the past while, stepping in and handling things with his usual eye for detail and incredible organization. He kept a close eye on Fee, as worried over her as I was. They spent a lot of time together while I was at work. She went with him when he had his cast removed, a simple sling replacing the heavy plaster. He spent hours talking with her. Given the situation, I had bitten the bullet and hired a temp to get me through for a couple of weeks so that Rene could help Fee. She was more important than my business.

"Fee, dear, how about some soup? You haven't eaten all day," he encouraged her.

She sighed, passing a hand over her face. She shook her head, her gaze drifting to mine. I met her tired eyes with my own. Neither of us was sleeping now. She was restless and unable to settle, and I was tense and worried. Without her by my side, sleep didn't come.

Fee sat up, the blanket slipping from her shoulders. She cleared her throat. "Halton," she began.

I sat across from her.

"Right here, Fee."

She reached for my hand, and I grasped it, holding it tight.

"I need your attorney hat on for a while," she stated.

"Okay."

She looked between Rene and me. "You've both been so amazing. Thank you for everything." She drew in a deep breath. "I've made a decision. Well, two, actually."

"Okay," I said, a pit of worry forming in my stomach.

"I need you to support me and act as my attorney for both of my decisions."

I nodded, somehow knowing I wasn't going to like either one.

"I need you to work with Jonas and do whatever it is you need to do to settle this issue with Connie. But I don't want the insurance money or the value of Scott's shares in the practice—or whatever will be left once Scott's debts are paid off."

She held up her hand before I could protest. "I don't want it," she repeated. "I got my settlement, and it's done."

"Fee—" I began. Scott's girlfriend would use the money to further her drug habit. I had no doubt of that.

She shook her head. "Hear me out. I want the money to go into a trust fund and do some good. Something that will help people struggling with addiction." She ran a hand over her head. "Settle with Connie. I know she wants money. Give it to her—get her out of my life."

I met Rene's eyes. He dipped his chin, telling me silently not to argue with Fee. I could understand her feelings, but part of me wanted her to have all the money so she would never have to worry again. But I knew I needed to respect her wishes.

"I'll work with Jonas. You don't have to worry about it, okay? I'll handle it, and you'll only have to sign some papers." It was much more complex than that, but I didn't want her to stress.

"Thank you," she breathed out, relieved I wasn't arguing with her.

"What is your second decision, Fee?" Rene asked.

She smiled, a genuine smile this time, and lifted her head, squaring her shoulders. "I'm buying a house."

Rene's answering grin was wide. "The bungalow we looked at the other day? With the porch?"

"Yes."

"Excellent choice."

It was all I could do not to gape at them. I had no idea they had been looking at houses together for Fee to purchase. Neither of them had said anything.

Fee nodded. "I made an offer, and the one condition was an inspection. It's empty and I have the money, so I asked for a two-week closing date."

My gaze flew between them. Two weeks? Fee was moving out in two weeks? The words were out of my mouth before I could stop them.

"Are you sure? Why are you rushing into this?"

Rene kicked my shin, and Fee looked confused. "I love this house. It's perfect for me, and why should I wait?"

I wanted to scream that she had to wait because I wasn't ready to let her go. But I couldn't. I knew I couldn't hold her back. I had set the rules, and she was following them.

I knew our time was coming to a close.

The saturation point had been reached for us both. I had to ignore the little voice in my head telling me, for the first time ever, I was the one not ready to let go.

I forced a smile to my face.

"You shouldn't."

Two weeks later, I followed Fee around her house, trying to show some enthusiasm for her new place. It was a great little house. Two bedrooms, a third room that would work well as an office. It had a well-appointed kitchen with a walk-out to a deck and a grassy, fenced-in yard. There was a new porch on the front of the house, well-built and covered. The two bathrooms were updated and modern, one with a large tub I knew Fee would use a lot. She liked the one in my condo. The basement was finished with a large TV area and a workout space. Set in a quiet neighborhood, the house was solid, and she would, no doubt, be happy here.

That was what I wanted, wasn't it?

I had done my job. I was working behind the scenes with Jonas to move along Scott's estate as fast as possible. I involved Fee as little as I could, knowing it upset her. It was complicated and messy, but eventually, it would be done. I wished I had gotten her more in her settlement or she had agreed to take at least the life insurance money, but it was Fee who made the final decision. Invested well, the money I had gotten her would make sure she wouldn't have to worry about her future. She had a good head on her shoulders, and I knew she would be fine.

So why was I so pissed off?

She turned to me. "Well?"

"It's great, Fee."

Her excited expression fell. "What's wrong?"

"Nothing. It's a great house. I saw all the reports and the inspection document. You chose well."

She took my hand and dragged me down the hall. The master bedroom was large and bright. A new bed sat in the middle of the room—one of the few pieces of furniture in the house. There was nothing else—not even a headboard. Just the bed. She had told me she planned on painting and creating each room gradually.

"Scott had the other house done—I had no say. I never liked it. I want to feel this house and make it mine," she had explained to me.

"I'm going to paint this room first. Green," she said, her voice excited. "A light, mossy green with white trim."

"Good choice." I indicated the bed. "King-size? You're kinda small for a king-size, Fee. Are you going to need steps to get to the mattress?"

She laughed. "Yes. I got a little stool." Then she became serious. "I know you like a king-size bed."

The back of my neck prickled. "What?"

She slipped a small box from her pocket and handed it to me.

"What is this?" I asked, eyeing it suspiciously.

"Take it and find out."

My anxiety grew. "I think I'm supposed to be the one to give you a housewarming gift, Fee. In fact, let me take you right now and pick something. Whatever you want."

She frowned, holding the small box. "What I want is for you to take this, Halton."

I accepted the box, my nerves tight. It was light and made a dull thump when I shook it. Fee laughed and perched against the edge of the bed. "It won't bite."

I opened the lid and lifted out a key. A shiny, silver key dangled from a chain with the initial *H* on it. Simple, heavy, and profound.

My eyes found hers. "What is this?"

"A key to the house."

"This house?"

"Yes, my house."

I closed my fingers around the key, holding it so tight, I felt the sharp edges digging into my skin.

"Why?" I asked. "Why would you give me a key?"

"So you can come and go as you need. It would be easier than having to call when you want to come over. I'm not just down the hall anymore."

"What are you talking about, Fee?"

She looked confused. "What am I... Halton, what's wrong?"

"What's wrong? What the hell are you thinking, Fee?" I didn't give her a chance to respond. "You can't give me a key. What do you think is going to happen? I'll stay here with you?"

She began to shake her head, and I kept going.

"We're not a couple. I don't do relationships—you knew this going in. I was your for now, not your forever."

"But I thought—"

"You thought wrong." Suddenly, I was yelling. "Don't you get it, Fee? I am not *anyone's* forever. You deserve everything. A house, someone who can love you and give you a life. Love. Security."

She gaped, but I didn't stop. "That. Isn't. Me," I snarled.

I stepped forward, almost spitting in my rage. "Don't you dare throw your life away on me. I didn't fight to get you free from that asshole for you to pin your hopes on the likes of me. There is no future for us."

"I'm not asking anything of you, Halton. I'm simply giving you a key."

I flung the key. It bounced off the wall, hitting the hardwood floor with a loud clunk. "So, what? I can come and go, fuck you on occasion? Drift in and out of your life and drain you of everything good? I can't give you anything else!" I grabbed her shoulders. "Stop it, Fee!"

She shook her head, and I knew she wasn't going to accept what had to happen.

I opened my mouth and sealed my fate.

I pressed my fingers into her arms and met her gaze. "If you do this, then you'll become the whore you never wanted to be with me."

Her gaze widened. Tears filled her eyes. "Get out."

I turned and walked away, pausing at the door, turning. "You have a job if you want one, and I will always be there if you need anything."

She turned away. "I don't need anything from you."

I nodded. "Good decision."

I left her.

A noise broke through the fog in my mind. I peeled open one eye then slammed it shut as pain drove through my head like a freight train.

I groaned and rolled over, cursing as I fell off the sofa.

Why the hell wasn't I in bed?

I sat up, clutching my head. A steady drum beat inside it, making me desperate for Tylenol. And water.

I was parched.

It was the sound of a key in the lock that made me raise my head. Only two people in the world beside me had a key to my place.

Fee and Rene.

I tried to focus my eyes on the figure moving across the room.

"Fee?" I croaked, hopeful.

"Try again."

"Rene," I sighed, hanging my head. I couldn't deal with him right now. "Go away."

"Nope." He sat down and grimaced. "Jesus, Halton, you stink of bourbon."

I glanced blearily at the coffee table and the almost empty bottle lying on its side slowly dripping liquor onto my hardwood floor. I had grabbed the bottle with one intent—to get drunk and forget.

I got drunk. But I didn't forget.

"I didn't want to waste the scotch," I muttered.

"Uh-huh." Rene leaned back on the chair. "Are you aware it's Monday morning? Midmorning?"

"What?" I scrambled to my feet, groaning at the pain in my head and the way my stomach lurched at my sudden movement.

"I canceled your day. It's all rescheduled over the next two days. You're going to have to work extra to get it all done." Rene stood. "In the meantime, go and shower. I have a few things to say to you, and I don't feel like saying them while you smell like a cheap distillery and yesterday's pity party."

"I don't feel like a lecture," I fired back, trying to hold up my aching head. "I'm not a fucking child."

"Then stop acting like one." He turned and headed toward the kitchen. "You have half an hour. Be back here ready to listen or I quit."

I didn't move, and he turned, casting a glare that let me know how serious he was. "You're wasting time and my patience, Halton."

I spun on my heel, falling into the sofa before righting myself and heading to my room.

I had a feeling what he had to say wasn't going to make me feel any better.

I made the water as hot as I could bear, letting it rain down on my body and wash away the sweat and liquor of the past many hours. I washed my hair and soaped thoroughly but didn't bother trying to tame my beard. It could be bushy for the day. I dressed and returned to the living room, feeling somewhat better after swallowing three Tylenol before entering the shower. The brass band in my head had at least settled into a low, steady thump I could handle.

A cup of coffee waited for me, along with a plate of dry toast. I lifted the coffee, grateful for the bitter brew, but nudged the toast to the side. My stomach was already in knots and ready to heave—it didn't need the added incentive of food.

Rene allowed me a few moments of peace then sat forward, resting his arms on his thighs. I could see his injured arm still had a long way to go—it was smaller and didn't move as well as the other one, but I knew he would recover.

He cleared his throat, making me lift my gaze to his face. His countenance was serious, the look in his eyes one of disappointment.

Shame flooded my chest without him saying a word.

"Fee told you."

"Only that you broke things off with her. Unlike you, she was at the office this morning, prepared to act like a mature adult."

I shifted in my chair. I shouldn't be surprised by her generosity. But I had done more than just break things off with her. I had been horrible and said things I didn't mean so she would hate me.

"What are you doing, Halton? That woman is the best thing that has ever happened to you."

"Protecting her from me, Rene."

"Bullshit."

I stood, unable to sit and meet his eyes. His anger, I could handle. His disappointment, not so much.

"I'm incapable of maintaining a relationship. I'm emotionally stunted—you know that—I have nothing to offer."

He leaned back, straightening his pant leg. "Again, I call bullshit." He cocked his head to the side, studying me. "You want to know the real truth?"

With a huff, I sat down. "As if I have a choice."

He leaned forward, his gaze steady. "You're a fucking coward."

"*What?*"

"You heard me." He shook his head. "You think you're the first guy to feel doubts about love, Halton? That you are the only fucking man who has ever lived and wondered what the future would hold if he allowed his heart to feel? To worry about things?" He stuck his finger in my chest. "Coward."

I glared at him but held my tongue. I knew he was far from being finished.

"Yeah, you had a shit childhood. You have a rotten mother, and you lost your father too young. Your life was awful. I get it. But Halton, you are the one in control now. You are the one stopping yourself from finding happiness. There is no one to blame right now but yourself."

"I will fail. I already know that."

He shook his head, his anger showing. "You know nothing of the sort. The Halton I know has never failed at anything he set his mind to. You're the one stopping this from happening. This is on you—no one else."

I stared, silent. His words echoed in my head, but I knew he wasn't done.

"One of the things I have always admired about you is your honesty, Halton. But right now, you're lying to yourself and to me. You're not afraid to fail. You're afraid to *feel*. I saw something in you these past weeks with Fee I was afraid I would never see. I saw you *live*. Actually fucking live. Not work all the time and take pills to find a few hours of sleep. You laughed. Smiled more. Touched another human. Cared for her. You were prepared to do anything in order to make sure she was okay—even risk your career for her." He held up his hand, stopping me from replying. "Don't give me the bullshit about it being your job. I've been with you for years, and I've seen you do your job. Go above and beyond for your clients, but not like this, Halton. Not the way you were with Fee."

There was a beat of silence. He narrowed his gaze, hunching closer.

"The way you looked at her. The way your face changed when she would walk into the room—how you responded to her in every way. That wasn't an attorney with a client, or a boss with an employee. That was a man in love." He sat back. "Why are you throwing that away?"

I could only shake my head, unable to speak.

Rene's voice grew solemn. Low and serious.

"How do you think I felt at eighteen when I got Sally pregnant? I had no choice but to grow up fast. Accept my responsibilities. Act like an adult. I was scared shitless about the future, but I did it. I worked and went to school. Life wasn't easy. Hell, we were still kids, but we made it work. I became a father when most of my friends were going to university and partying. I was home, changing diapers. I worked hard, and so did my wife. We relied on each other, and against all odds, we made it." He sighed. "I was scared every day for years, Halton. Worried if I had done the right thing. If my carelessness had messed up not only our lives, but my son's as well. But I had Sally, and she was my rock." A tear ran down his cheek, and he brushed it away. "I miss her every day, but I will never regret taking that chance with her and making a great life. You are throwing away the best thing that has ever happened to you."

"This is different."

"Is it? Is it really? Aren't you refusing to take a chance? To trust someone in a way you have never trusted before? Fee is not your mother, Halton. Her love doesn't come with pain and games. What you see is what you get with her. And what I see when I look at her is a woman deeply in love with a man and wanting to help him."

"I don't love her. I don't love anyone. That's the point," I snapped. "Why can't you accept that about me? I care for people. Yes, some more than others, but I am incapable of love. Emotional attachments aren't for me."

He pursed his lips and sat back, crossing his legs. He regarded me for a moment and I waited for his BS comment again, but instead, he tilted his head.

"All right."

I was surprised by his remark.

"The lecture is over, then?"

"I have one question, and I want an honest answer. Then I'll drop it."

I sat back, mirroring his pose. "Ask me."

"Consider yourself under oath, Halton. I am asking for brutal honesty."

I waved my hand. "Ask."

"If you're incapable of love and you have no deep emotional attachment to Fee, why did you drink yourself into oblivion this weekend after you broke it off with her?"

I blinked. Then, again. Rene's intense gaze never wavered.

I swallowed the sudden dryness in my throat.

"She was awesome in bed. I'll miss the sex."

He stood, looking down at me. "I have seen and heard you do a lot of questionable things, Halton—" he huffed out a disgusted breath "—but this is the first time I have ever been ashamed of you." He walked to the door. "Straighten yourself out and get your ass into the office tomorrow. I am not covering for you again."

The door slammed behind him, the sound making me wince.

The silence that followed his departure, however, was far louder.

I was in the office early on Tuesday, wanting to be prepared for whatever hell the day held for me. Between Rene's anger and Fee's hurt, I wasn't sure how I would handle myself.

I heard them come in, chatting like old friends. Not long after, Rene brought me in a coffee and sat down, his tablet in hand, his voice calm, his demeanor the same as usual, although I detected a trace of coldness that hadn't existed until now.

"We need to go over your schedule." He turned and called over his shoulder. "Fee, a moment please, dear."

I braced myself, unsure how this was going to play out. Fee came in, her hair swept up, a gray suit showing off her shapely body. She sat down, offering me a cool smile.

"Hello, Hal. I hope you're feeling better today."

Hal. She called me Hal.

Somehow, I didn't like hearing her call me that name. But I forced a return smile and played along with their game.

"Yes, better, *Fee.* Thank you."

She didn't react to the emphasis I put on her name. She crossed her legs, the skirt riding up and showing her dimpled knees. I recalled kissing those dimples. Tracing my finger around the edges as I gripped her knees, spreading her open while I licked her to orgasm.

I had to avert my eyes.

The next twenty minutes were surreal. It was as if nothing had occurred. We went through my schedule, switching appointments, adjusting times, and making sure we were all on the same page. Fee didn't talk much, but she jotted down notes, offered a few suggestions, and kept her gaze fixed firmly on Rene.

I couldn't stop looking at her.

She was pale, and she looked as tired as I felt. I wanted to touch her, ask her if she was okay, but I knew I no longer had the right.

When the meeting was over, she stood and went into the library. Rene followed, shutting the door between us.

It remained closed the rest of the week.

I only saw Fee if she was at Rene's desk or passing through the reception area. She somehow always managed to drop off my lunch at my desk while I was on the phone. She was professional, polite, and impersonal. Exactly the way I would want an extra assistant in the office to act.

I hated it. Every single fucking minute of it.

By Friday, I was tense and agitated. I spent the afternoon closed in judge's chambers, shredding an asshole who was trying to take his child away from my client to be vindictive. I let my anger loose, and by the time we were done and I had presented my case, not only did Vivian have custody, her ex-husband was paying through the nose for his stupid stunt. All my aggression went into my arguments, and they were on point, succinct, and dripping with rage.

Back at my office building, I rested my head against the cool metal wall of the elevator, grateful I was the lone occupant. I was exhausted. My insomnia had returned with a vengeance. Before Fee, I had managed a few hours a night. Now I was lucky to get fifteen-minute naps spaced out by long hours of pacing, trying to exhaust myself. I knew I would have to swallow some pills this weekend to get some rest. They would leave me groggy and unable to function well the next morning, but by Saturday afternoon, I would be better. I hated taking them, but at this point, I had no choice.

I somehow doubted Fee would offer to let me sleep beside her, even if I asked. She had looked tired this morning, the dark circles under her eyes almost as bad as mine. She had still smiled that distant smile I hated and said good morning, before going into the library and shutting the door in our shared wall.

I walked into the office, partially relieved, partially disappointed when I found only Rene there. He was on the phone, his gaze watchful as I went to my desk, sitting down heavily. I noticed the door was now open between the library and my office and the top of Fee's desk was empty and spotless except for the lamp on the corner she liked to use. She must have cleaned it off for the weekend. As I went through the stack of messages on my desk, my gaze kept drifting to the empty desk—somehow, it seemed odd to me.

Rene came in and slid a tray onto the corner of my desk. I picked up the cup of coffee and attacked the sandwich. I was starving. He sat across from me, discussing the busy schedule I had next week.

"You are booked solid. Including three attorneys who you want to interview to join you. I have those scheduled in the early evenings."

I nodded around a mouthful of pastrami.

"I spoke with Bentley earlier. The office on the other side of the library is about to become vacant. He said he had no issues adding it to your current lease. We could add another set of doors in the corner and expand easily."

I frowned and swallowed. "But Fee's desk is there."

He waved his hand. "Not an issue. I looked at the plans. Lots of room for an assistant's desk in the new space. Bentley offered to send over some ideas. He has Liv and Van working on it already. You can look over the drawings next week."

Liv and Van were two of my favorite people at BAM. I had helped them on a few occasions—once when her ex tried to take their daughter, whom he never wanted, from Liv, and with the adoptions of their two children. I was even godfather to their daughter Amelia. Why they had granted the honor to me, I still hadn't figured out, but I had to admit I was fond of the child. All their children, actually. They were a great family. I had every confidence I would like their ideas since they knew me so well and what I liked.

"Okay. That's great." I scrubbed my face.

"You look exhausted."

I lifted one shoulder. "I am."

"Have you slept at all this week?"

"Maybe three hours in total," I admitted.

He shook his head, his look saying it all. I knew I had done it to myself.

"You need to sleep, Halton. I assume you'll be taking your prescription tonight?"

"Yeah."

"I will check on you in the morning."

I met his eyes, seeing only sadness and worry in them.

"Thanks, Rene. I appreciate it."

He stood. "Don't work too late."

"I won't. I'm going to grab a bite at the bar later and head home by nine."

Pausing, he held the back of the chair but didn't say anything for a moment. "All right."

Before he could leave, I had to ask. "Fee left already? Was she okay?"

"She had an appointment."

"Ah." Then before I could stop myself, the words were out. "Why is her desk so clean?"

He stopped at the door, regarding me sadly. "Because she left, Halton. She found another job, and she will not be returning. She asked me to wish you much luck."

He turned and walked away.

I was out of my seat in a second, following him.

"*What?* Why did she leave? Where did she go?"

"Does it matter?"

"Of course, it matters," I snapped.

He slid his coat around his shoulders, the movement still jerky and slow. "She is going to work for BAM."

"*What the hell?*" I yelled.

He held up his hand before I could continue.

"Reid was here yesterday, and he mentioned they're so busy that Sandy required an assistant of her own. I called her and recommended Fee. They met last night, and Sandy hired her immediately. She gave me her notice today. I, of course, waived her two-week notice period, so she could start fresh next week. I thought it was for the best." He eyed me. "It wasn't as if she had a contract or anything holding her here."

"You *recommended* her? Why the hell would you do that? She was invaluable here!"

He perched on the edge of his desk. "Yes, she was, and I will miss her immensely. But the fact is that the situation wasn't going to work, and we all knew that. Given the tension between you two, it was inevitable this would happen."

"I thought everything was fine!" I protested, knowing my words were a lie but spouting them anyway.

Rene stood, shaking his head. "That seems to be a constant issue with you these days, Halton. Unless it's for your clients, your thought process, frankly, is fucked. You have no one to blame for this but yourself. Fee will be happier working in a place where she isn't reminded of her mistakes every time she sees you."

His choice of words stung.

"Mistakes? What, now—I'm a *mistake?*"

"Hiring you as her attorney, no. Working here, no. Falling in love with you and thinking that somehow, with enough patience, she would show you that love is real and good, yes. As I said before, your determination not to try made sure that was a wasted effort. I hope she can move past you. I really do—she deserves it."

"So much for loyalty," I spat out.

He tugged on his sleeves. "Oh, you have my loyalty. You will always have that. But I have come to see even I don't rank high enough for you to truly consider me worthy of your love."

"What?"

He studied me for a moment. "I love you as my own son, Halton. I have all these years. I always thought, in some way, I was like a father to you. That I meant something to you—stupidly, I thought enough of our relationship to think you loved me in your own way, even though you can't express it. But you have insisted time and again you're incapable of any sort of love. So I have to assume my affection is one-sided and act accordingly. You have my loyalty and I will continue to care, but like Fee, I cannot allow my heart to feel more, knowing the sentiment will never be returned."

He strode to the door, looking back at me. "And that, more than anything, saddens me. You have such a capacity for love, Halton. Everyone can see it but you. The only person who thinks you're unworthy or incapable of it is you. It truly breaks my heart."

He left, once again leaving me alone with my thoughts.

They were loud enough to fill the silence that surrounded me.

I tossed my phone to the side, my mood even darker after accepting a call from my mother. After our conversation, it would be the last one I ever accepted.

Rain hit the windows, a steady beat of drops. It had gotten harder as the evening grew longer, the darkness settling across the sky. I stared out the window, hearing the distant rumble of thunder growing closer.

When it fully hit, the storm was going to be violent.

Much the way the storm in my head felt.

I set down my scotch and picked up my phone, dialing a number with impatient fingers.

"I don't want to hear it," Bentley stated, not bothering with hello. "Unless you're calling to thank me for the extra office space, shut it. She came to us. All I did was talk to her. Sandy made the decision, and frankly, I think she'll be a huge asset here."

"Change her mind."

Bentley laughed. "Who? Sandy? Fee?"

"Both of them."

"Hal, I don't know the whole story, but I know enough. You need the separation. She needs a fresh start." He lowered his voice. "Isn't that why you fought so hard for her? To give her a fresh start?"

"Yes."

"Then let her go. Give it to her."

I looked around the office, needing to say the words to someone. Needing to get them out before I buried them so deep, they would never escape. They bubbled and pricked at my throat, needing to be said.

"I-I think I fucked up, Bent."

"With Fee?"

I thought of the pain in Rene's voice. The look on his face when he left the office. I realized with utter clarity, I was going to lose everyone who was truly important to me. I was letting fear win. I was allowing my past to dictate my future. If I didn't stop it now, I would regret it. I knew it with every fiber of my being.

"With a lot of things."

"Then un-fuck them."

"I don't know how."

"Yeah, you do, Hal. Suck it up and do it." He paused. "When I fell for Emmy, it was hard to admit I could need someone the way I needed her. Aiden almost lost Cami before he was able to admit his feelings. Maddox went through hell, but he refused to lose Dee. It's not a bloody easy thing to do, but trust me, the risk is worth it. Especially with someone with a heart like Fee's. In the short time I spoke to her, I could tell she was special."

"She is."

"I could see she was hurting, but she had nothing but positive things to say about you, Hal. She spoke of your work ethic and how you helped her. The way you help other people. The compassion you show." He paused. "Maybe it's time you show yourself some of the same compassion."

I swallowed, unable to form the right retort. His words astounded me, but they shouldn't have been a surprise. Fee's nature was one of sweetness and warmth. She always saw the positive.

"Maybe you're right."

"Of course I am. Think hard, Hal. Don't mess around with her—I think she's been through enough."

"I agree."

"Then tread carefully. But I'm not reneging on my offer to her. And you're welcome about the office space. You can take me to lunch next week, once you get your head out of your ass."

He hung up.

I stared out the window, my life drifting by in random bursts of memories. My mother and her cruelty. My father's attempts to be what I needed, then his despondency when he realized he would never win and giving up. Choosing alcohol over me.

Both of them abandoned me in their own way. They left scars I never allowed to heal. When Fee was close, they began to knit closed, but now that she was gone, they were torn open, bleeding profusely.

I looked around the office, thinking of next week—next month— next year. No Fee peeking at me over the top of her laptop. No stolen, sweet kisses. None of her sass or the perfect way she slid into the chair across from me, crossing her legs in the way she knew teased and taunted me.

No Fee beside me at night. No gift of restful slumber or waking up to her the next morning. No one to share the odd moments of my day I wanted to talk about. To sit with on the sofa, not saying a word, but sharing so much at the same time with a simple touch.

The thought of not ever feeling her touch, not ever seeing her again caused me physical pain. I blinked away the sudden moisture in my eyes.

And Rene. I did think of him as a father figure. He was a prime example of how a man should be with his family. The thought that he felt I didn't care as much for him as he did for me rankled, but I knew I deserved his anger.

I thought of his insistence that I was capable of real, honest emotion.

Love.

Was it possible I loved Fee?

I rubbed my chest, the ache that had been building all night burning and relentless. If knowing I would never see Fee, never touch her again, felt like this, then Rene was right.

I had been fooling myself.

I did love her. As terrifying as the thought was, she had become the center of my world. Her presence soothed me, her touch anchored me, and her smile lit my world ablaze.

I had screwed up in horrendous fashion. In trying to stop myself from being hurt, I had hurt those I deeply cared for. I was so afraid of love and the pain, I didn't see I was causing myself even greater pain. And by acting the way I had been, I had become the sort of person I fought against daily.

I made others feel less. As if *they* were not enough, when in fact, they were everything.

The simple reality of those words was astounding.

I grabbed the phone, my fingers shaking as I pressed the numbers.

"Halton," Rene answered wearily. "It's eleven p.m. What is so important?"

"I love you, old man. You're like a fucking father to me, and I'm sorry for all this shit."

There was silence, then he spoke, his voice wary.

"Have you been drinking again?"

"No." I barked out a laugh. "I've been thinking about what you said. About what an ass I've been."

"Well, hallelujah. Miracles do happen."

"I'm serious. You're a vital part of my life, Rene. You mean more than you know. More than I can properly express." I swallowed. "You're the family I chose for myself."

Rene's voice was raspy when he finally replied.

"You have no idea what that means to me."

"Yeah, I do. I'm long overdue in saying it. I'm sorry."

"Just full of apologies tonight, aren't you?"

"Necessary ones."

"Apology accepted."

"Thank you." The sudden rumble of thunder made me jump. "Shit."

"What?"

"The storm—Fee hates them. They scare her, and she's alone."

"You're still in the office I presume?"

"Yes."

"There may be a spare key in my top right desk drawer Fee gave me for emergencies," Rene said.

I sucked in a sharp breath. "I'm not sure she wants to see me."

"Try, Halton. Take the key and go to her. She needs you and, frankly, you need her even more. Grovel if you have to."

Another rumble sounded, the sky lighting up, bright and vivid. Fee would be terrified.

I stood. "Well, it is the night for apologies. "

"That's the spirit."

"I meant it, Rene." I remembered the words I had heard Bentley say so often and never understood until this moment. "You are my family."

"Go get your girl, Halton. Allow yourself to be happy."

I found the key, holding it up like a trophy. "On it."

I couldn't call Fee. She had given Rene her cell phone and told him she would be getting a new one from BAM. It was in the drawer next to the key, and I shoved it into my pocket. I would give it back to her if she allowed me to do so.

I drove as fast as I could. The streets were mostly deserted in the dreadful weather, and I made it to her house in record time. I pulled in the driveway and hurried to the door, ignoring the rain soaking into my suit. The power was out on the street, all the houses dark. I used the flashlight on my phone to light my way. I knocked, but there was no answer, which didn't surprise me. Inserting the key, I paused briefly, unsure as to what her reaction would be when she saw me. Inside, I slipped off my shoes, calling her name so I didn't frighten her any further. The thunder echoed in the empty rooms as I hurried down the hall.

"Fee!" I shouted, panicked when she hadn't replied. "Love, where are you?"

"Halton?" her anxious voice finally responded. I rushed to her room, holding my phone high, the light guiding me to her. She was on her bed, sitting in the middle, wrapped in a comforter. Her hands gripped the edges, keeping it tight to her body.

"Wh-what are you doing here?"

"I came for you."

In one fast movement, she lunged off the bed, and I caught her in my arms, feeling the tremors racing through her body.

"It's okay, love. I've got you." I pressed my lips to her head, inhaling the fragrant scent of her hair. "I'm not going anywhere."

"I know it's not forever, but I need you," she whimpered as another long roll of thunder shook the walls.

I tilted up her chin, meeting her eyes in the dim light cast by my phone. "It is forever, if you'll have me, Fee."

Her chin trembled in my grip. "What?"

"Forgive me for my actions. Forgive me for being a coward. Let me be with you, Fee. Tonight. Tomorrow. Always."

Tears coursed down her cheeks.

I sank onto the bed, holding her tight. She wrapped her arms around my neck, silent sobs shaking her shoulders. I placed my lips to her ear.

"I love you, FeeNelly. I've never loved anyone until now, but I love you. I want to be with you."

She looked up, her cheeks wet. "So you can sleep?"

I smiled, wiping her face. "So I can live."

"Why?" she whispered, doubt still coloring her voice. "How?"

"I realized I was hurting you. Hurting Rene." A sigh rumbled through my chest. "I was denying myself something I wanted but was too afraid to accept."

"Tell me."

I met her gaze. "I am worthy of love. Of being loved and giving it." I gripped her tighter. "I want your love, Fee. I want you."

She cupped my face, not speaking. Turning my head, I kissed her palm and pressed her hand into my skin.

"You told me once you thought everyone had a little perfection inside them. Let me love you, Fee. If you're inside my heart, then I finally have my perfection. You're it."

"Halton..."

"Tell me I'm not too late. Forgive me."

She held me tighter, brushing her lips to mine. "Forgiven." She kissed me, whispering against my mouth, "I love you, Halton Smithers. I love you. I love you. I love you. I'm going to say it until you're sick of hearing it."

"Not gonna happen, Fee. I'll never tire of those words," I whispered back. "I love you."

The storm passed, but Fee and I remained locked together on her bed. I had only moved to shed my wet suit then lay beside her, holding her close. As exhausted as I was, as we both were, I couldn't sleep. I had too much to say.

"I've been such an ass."

"You were trying to protect yourself."

I laughed, kissing her forehead. "I didn't need protection from you, Fee. Or Rene."

She snuggled closer. "You weren't ready to admit that yet, Halton." She tipped up her head. "What changed?"

"What Rene said. The thought of never seeing you." I swallowed. "A call I got from my mother."

"Oh."

I sighed. "She wanted money. She didn't say hello or even pretend. She just wanted money. When I said no, she wasn't happy."

"And?"

"I asked her why she never loved me enough. Why she kept me

away from my father. She said it was to prove a point. When I told her that it was her fault he became a drunk and ruined my life, she laughed. It hit me right then, she had no empathy. For my father—for me. It terrified me more than her illness. I never wanted to become that callous, and by refusing to admit my feelings for people, I was doing exactly that. And by continuing to be in contact with her, I was letting her continue to hurt me." I ran my hand down Fee's back in a long, slow motion. "I don't need people who hurt in my life. I need people like you. It was time to cut off the past and move forward." I met her eyes in the dimness. "With you."

"I'm sorry she hurt you. And I'm sorry you had to cut ties."

I shrugged. "Actually, it felt good. I don't owe her anything. She thinks I do, and I'd let her make me feel the same way. It's done."

"You don't owe anyone anything, Halton, except yourself."

"What do I owe myself?"

She cupped my cheek. "To be happy."

"I need you for that to happen, Fee."

"You have me."

"Can I stay?" I asked, my heart in my throat.

"You want to stay with me? Here?"

"I don't want to go back to the condo. I'm tired of being alone. I want to be with you."

"Yeah." She tightened her hold on my face. "Yeah, you can stay—for as long as you want."

"I want it all."

"What are you saying?"

"I lied to you. Weeks ago. I don't want to be your right now, Fee. I want to be your forever. If you let me."

"My forever," she repeated.

I kissed her palm. "Marry me."

Shock rendered her speechless.

I held her hand over my heart. "This is useless without you. Be my perfect spot forever, FeeNelly."

"Halton," she whispered.

"Please."

Her answer was as simple and perfect as she was to me.

"Yes."

I pulled her close, kissing her with everything I had in me. Finally free to let myself feel the emotion of loving her.

My Fee.

Moments passed of relearning her in a different language entirely. One of love.

The last of our clothing disappeared with gentle hands. There was nothing rushed or urgent. Long, slow passes of my tongue on hers. Tender sweeps of my fingers along her silky skin. There was a low hum in my body, a need for her I couldn't explain. I couldn't get close enough. I couldn't touch her enough or taste her enough to satisfy my craving for her. No matter what I did, I needed more.

I needed her.

I was cradled between her legs and our gazes locked as I slid inside her, my body easing once we were joined. With a low groan, I buried my face into her fragrant neck.

"Welcome home," she murmured.

Fusing our lips together, I moved inside her slowly. We were connected from hip to neck, our skin molded together so close, it was as if we were one. I kept my movements easy, our hips never separating as I rode her. Her tender touch made me shiver.

"How do you convey so much with your touch?" I asked, my gaze locked on hers. "How did I not feel your love until now?"

"You weren't ready."

"Don't ever stop."

She pulled me close, her mouth a breath away from mine.

"Never."

I loved her with everything I had. My body worshiped hers. My words expressed it. My heart beat her name.

My orgasm washed over me, slow, deep, and powerful. She tightened around me, calling my name. We crested together, our hearts echoing in the passion of the moment.

I rolled away, pulling her close and holding her tight. "I love you."

"Hmm," she whispered. "Always, Halton. I'm yours."

With a contented sigh, I let sleep take me, safe in the knowledge I had her beside me.

"When are you coming home?" Fee's voice was rough. She'd had the flu the past couple of days, and I hated leaving her alone at home, but the office was crazy.

In the month we'd officially been living together, a lot of changes had happened. I'd hired another lawyer—a woman named Lydia Watson, who had been far and away the most impressive in her interview—even astonishing Rene with her ethics and desire to help people. She was currently working in the library, but Van was busy in the office next door, and soon, she would have her own space.

I let Rene choose the new assistant. Fee felt it best to still work for BAM, thinking we needed that separation. I hated it and had tried to persuade her to change her mind, but she was adamant. I had to admit, the young man, Clark, who Rene had hired, was excellent at his job. Rene enjoyed bossing him around a great deal.

The office was busy, productive, and hummed all day and often well into the evening. Luckily, Bentley's office wasn't far away. So on occasion I got to see Fee during the day for lunch, and she often came after work to help me out. Those were my favorite days.

"Another hour, love. I promise. I'll bring home some soup?"

"Yeah," she said. "I feel a little better. I hope you don't get it."

I chuckled. "Since both Clark and Rene had it, I'm shocked it skipped Lydia and me and went for you."

"I guess I hugged them too much last week."

"You had best save your hugs for me, then," I growled playfully.

She laughed. "Incorrigible."

"Yep. Mine."

She sighed. "Come home soon, counselor. I miss you."

Her words made my chest warm the way they usually did.

"Soon."

I hung up and dug into my pocket, bringing out the small velvet box. For the hundredth time, I opened it and stared at the ring. The beautiful emerald sparkled under the light, the diamonds surrounding it brilliant. Bentley had sent me to a friend of his, and she helped me design and choose the perfect gemstone and setting. I wanted an emerald because of Fee's lovely eyes and the warmth of the color. Diamonds seemed too cold for her. I was sure Fee would love it, but I hadn't given it to her yet for some reason.

She had already said yes, so the ring was a simple formality, but I was still nervous. Rene found it amusing, and I knew he was anxious for me to give the ring to Fee. I would as soon as she was over this flu bug. It had been a twenty-four-hour thing for him and Clark, but for Fee, it had been a few days.

A throat clearing made me look up. Reid was in my doorway, his laptop under his arm, looking oddly nervous. I was surprised to see him, and for some reason, his unease put me on edge.

"Hey."

He came in, shutting my door, and then sat across from me.

I slid the ring box back into my pocket. "What's going on?"

He sighed and leaned forward. "I was cleaning up my drive today —deleting files and freeing up space. I saw something I thought you needed to know."

"What?"

He hesitated, then opened his laptop. His anxiety made me tense, and I frowned as he spun the screen in my direction.

"There was a file from Scott's computer. I hadn't noticed it until today, and it caught my eye as I was deleting them. I opened it and read it. It seemed—well, it seemed important."

I pulled the laptop close and read what looked like a medical report. I read it again, then met Reid's eyes.

"Holy fuck."

He raised his eyebrows in agreement with my statement.

"Scott had a vasectomy? He told Fee his tests came back fine. How is that possible?"

Reid tugged a hand through his hair. "I'll give you the gist of what I discovered. Scott hired a doctor, who has since lost his license. The report was false. Scott's vasectomy happened six months before they had their tests." He met my gaze. "Fee's test was falsified as well. It appears Scott had no desire for kids but didn't want to tell Fee, so he lied."

I froze. "That bastard made her think it was all her."

"Yeah."

"Goddamn asshole," I fumed.

"Ah, Hal?"

"What?" I growled, wishing Scott were still alive so I could kill him all over again.

"I don't want to get personal here, but doesn't Fee supposedly have the stomach flu?"

Supposedly?

"Yes."

"Ah, do you use protection?"

I blinked at his question and was about to tell him to mind his own business when the lightbulb went off. Fee wasn't infertile, and we'd been having unprotected sex for weeks.

She'd been ill longer than Rene. Her symptoms were somewhat different.

It wasn't the fucking flu.

I stood so fast, my chair toppled over.

"Holy fuck. I have to go."

He laughed and stood, then shouted at me before I reached the door.

"Hal!"

I spun around. "What?"

He held out the ring box. "You might need this."

I grabbed the box that had fallen from my pocket. "Thanks."

He winked. "Congrats—on *all* the news."

I tore out of the office, running as quickly as I could.

How the hell was I going to tell Fee?

I found her on the bathroom floor, resting her head on the cold tub beside the toilet. She lifted her head wearily as I rushed in, offering me a small smile.

"It came back."

I lifted her into my arms, cradling her close. "Sorry, love."

She pushed away. "Ugh. I smell awful."

"I don't care."

"I do. Let me clean up."

I stood behind her as she brushed her teeth and washed her face. She was pale, her eyes exhausted.

My thoughts were rampant. I had to tell her that her dead ex-husband was a lying sack of shit, and then follow it up with, "And by the way you may be pregnant since I fuck you every chance I get. I stopped and got a pregnancy test—wanna pee on the stick?"

I chuckled dryly as I wondered if she'd knee me in the balls or just yell.

She looked at me in the mirror with a puzzled look.

"I look so bad, you're laughing?"

I wrapped my arms around her, tugging her back to my chest. "You're beautiful. I'm laughing at my own thoughts right now."

"Did you bring the ginger ale?"

"And crackers."

"Crackers?"

"Ah, Rene said they were good for nausea."

He had said a lot of things when I called him from the car. He had also laughed so hard, I was certain he was crying.

"Oh, Halton. You have no idea. Your life—" his laughter rang out again "—oh, how your life is about to change. I am going to enjoy the hell out of this."

"Rene, how am I going to handle this? I never planned on children!"

He sobered. "You never planned on falling in love either. That turned out pretty damn well, I would say. Tell me, Halton, what are you feeling right now?"

I took the exit for the house. The one I shared with Fee—our home. I thought of his question. Hearing the news, I had felt no anger or stress. None of the nonsense about not bringing a child into this world. Fee and I would make sure they were okay. She would be sure I was okay. There was only worry about getting to Fee and the wonder of telling her. I knew once she got over the shock, she would be ecstatic.

"Happy and worried, I think."

"Worried about being a dad?"

"Worried about Fee. And yes, being a good dad."

"You will be, Halton. Put your mind to it the way you do everything else, and you'll be a great one."

"I want to be."

"Do you really think Fee or I would let you fail at something so important?"

He was right. With them in my life, I couldn't fail.

His words echoed in my head as I steered Fee to our bed and tucked her in. I sat beside her, offering her one of the cold ginger ales I had picked up for her.

She sipped it cautiously.

"Want a cracker?"

"Maybe later." She leaned her head against the pillows. She had about five of them piled up. She loved pillows. "I hope this ends soon. Why did Rene and Clark only have it for twenty-four hours?"

I tucked a strand of hair behind her ear. "It's not the flu, Fee."

"It's not?"

"No."

She rolled her eyes. "What is your diagnosis, Dr. Smithers?"

I cleared my throat. "Reid came to see me today. He noticed something in the files he had from Scott's computer. Something, ah, personal."

Her face grew even paler as I repeated what I had read and what Reid had told me.

She grew utterly still.

"Fee? Love? Did you hear me?"

She looked down at her stomach, laying her hand over it. The gesture made me smile.

"Fee?" I prompted.

"Will you leave me?" she asked.

I gaped at her, my eyes wide with alarm. "What? No! Never."

"But you said..." Her voice trailed off.

I gathered her hands together with mine. "I said a lot of senseless things before I finally got my head out of my ass. Forget them. They were spoken out of fear and stupidity."

Tears gathered in her eyes. "You want—you want to have a baby with me?"

"I want to have lots of babies with you. But we can start with this one."

She flung her arms around me, sobbing. I held her close, letting her cry. I ran my hand up and down her back, making shushing noises and rocking her. When her sobs stopped, I eased back and wiped her cheeks. I chuckled as she blew her nose.

"Okay, FeeNelly?"

She sniffled. "What do we do now?"

I rummaged in the bag and held up a box. "We pee on a stick."

The bathroom floor was cold. I sat with my back against the wall, Fee on my lap, with her holding the stick. It was turned over, and I was using my phone to time the results. I already knew what it as going to say, but I wanted to share this moment with her.

The buzzer went off, and Fee drew in a long breath. "I'm scared," she admitted.

I nudged her gently, resting my chin on her shoulder. "Nothing to be afraid of, Fee. I'm here." I covered her hand with mine. "I'll always be here."

She met my gaze and her shoulders relaxed. "Okay."

"On three," I whispered.

We turned over the stick, and the word PREGNANT stood out, vivid and clear.

"Wow," I murmured.

"You're going to be a daddy," Fee said, turning her head.

I kissed her. "You're going to be a mommy. A great one."

"I never thought I would get to be a mommy." Her eyes shone. "I can't believe it. It's not the flu, Halton. It's not the flu!"

I chuckled. "Nope. Not the flu. It's our baby." The words felt foreign to say, but strangely right.

"You're sure you're okay with this?" she asked, nervous.

I rested my cheek against hers. "You made a dream I didn't even know I had come true, Fee. I get to have my own family." I tightened my arms. "I will never leave you. Or let you down again. Either of you."

She pressed closer. "*You* are my dream, Halton. All my wishes came true."

"I have one more wish." I slid the tiny box into her hand. "One wish to make us both complete."

She looked down at the black velvet. Her hands shook as she opened it, a gasp escaping her mouth when she saw the ring.

"Wear my ring and be my wife," I murmured into her ear. "Be the mother of my children and my partner, Fee. Be my world, because you are my heart."

She turned her face, meeting my eyes.

"Yes."

I bent to kiss her and she gasped.

"What?"

"I'm gonna throw up."

She flung herself away, and I rubbed her back as she heaved, then I carried her back to bed, tucking her in and staring down at her. I stroked her forehead.

"Sleep, love. I'll be here when you wake up."

"I can't believe I barfed after you asked me to marry you."

I had to laugh. As far as marriage proposals went, I had a feeling ours was unique.

She fell asleep, exhausted. Her hand lay on top of the blanket, the emerald sparkling in the light. Her little raptor noises filled the room, making me smile.

She made me smile.

The light of my world. My partner in everything. Now for life.

Unique or not, I'd take it.

EPILOGUE

Four months later

Halton

I waited, anxious and excited, my foot tapping and my fingers clenching as the music began to play. Beside me, Rene chuckled and laid his hand on my shoulder.

"She's coming, Halton."

I had to smile. I knew she was, but it wasn't fast enough. I hadn't seen Fee since yesterday at lunch, and it was already seven p.m. It was the longest we'd been apart in months, and I hadn't been happy with that part of the plan but gave in when Fee said it was something she wanted. I found myself unable to ever say no to her.

It was one small tradition in our very untraditional relationship, she informed me. The plan had been she would spend the evening with Joanne and I was going to be with Rene, but our friends had other ideas.

The BAM boys—Bentley, Aiden, Maddox, Reid, Van, and even Jordan all showed up and dragged Rene and me to Maddox's favorite whiskey bar. Maddox had reserved an entire section and we sat around sipping whiskey, eating various platters of food Aiden ordered, and laughing. We were a loud, boisterous crew, and I actually enjoyed every moment. There was a lot of ribbing and marital advice offered—most of which I felt safe ignoring.

Especially from Aiden.

He leaned back in his chair, his big arm flung over the back. "As the longest married BAM man, lemme give you some advice."

Bentley rolled his eyes. "I asked Emmy first."

Aiden shook his head. "I made it legal before you."

Maddox smirked. "By a few months."

Aiden waved his hand. "Whatever. Still longer than both of you."

I met Van's amused gaze. The three of them constantly tried to outdo each other. It was amusing to watch, but I admired their relationship. I had never known three men to be as loyal and tight as they were with each other. Their friendship was solid, and it extended throughout their company and beyond. Once you were friends with them, you became part of their circle. I was grateful to be included.

I picked up my whiskey, enjoying the smoothness of the bottle we were sampling at the moment.

"Do impart your wisdom, Aiden."

He nodded sagely. "Always let her know who's the boss." He rolled his shoulders. "Cami knows who wears the pants in the family."

For a moment, everyone was silent. Then Maddox burst out laughing, and Bentley hung his head, his shoulders shaking in mirth. Reid laughed so hard, he almost fell off the low chair he was perched on. Van's head fell back as he guffawed, and even Jordan covered his eyes as he laughed. Rene simply shook his head, amusement written all over his face.

"What?" Aiden said.

"You're the boss when Cami tells you it's okay," Bentley informed him. "Which isn't often."

"What about you?" Aiden shot back.

Bentley lifted his shoulder. "Emmy owns me totally. What she says goes, and I'm good with that. Mad Dog?"

Maddox wiped his eyes. "Pretty much. What Dee says goes—well, most places." He winked suggestively. "There's one place I call the shots, but I'll keep that private."

Reid grinned. "I let Becca boss me around. I kinda like it."

We all laughed at that.

I turned my amused gaze to Van. I was the closest to him of the group. "What say you, Van? Liv the boss of the house?"

He shook his head slowly. "Nope."

"Really?" I asked, surprised.

He grinned into his whiskey. "Sammy is. What she says goes."

Everyone laughed at his droll statement. Sammy was Van's adopted daughter, and he adored her completely.

"Mila is second-in-command. Liv rounds them out." He concluded. "Reed and I just do what we're told." He clapped me on the shoulder. "It's easier that way, my friend. Go with the flow."

Bentley met my eyes, his gaze serious. "Ignore Tree Trunk here and listen to me, Halton. Love her. With everything in you. Emmy is the center of my world. She comes first. Over business, money, everything. If I lost all of it and only had her, I'd still have everything." His voice caught. "She is everything."

I nodded in understanding, my throat suddenly thick. Fee had already become more important to me than anything else. I would do anything for her happiness. Be whatever she needed me to be. Do whatever I had to do to keep her safe, happy, and beside me. I met Rene's dark eyes. He smiled in understanding, knowing what demons I had conquered to get to the point of admitting my love for Fee. He clapped me on the shoulder.

"What Bentley said, Halton. Love her."

That was what I planned on doing for the rest of my life.

Fee had her own surprise when Joanne drove her to a small restaurant in Mississauga and Fee walked in to find all the BAM women in attendance. Emmy, Cami, Dee, Becca, Liv, and Sandy were waiting with presents, and all the little canapés Fee craved constantly. Lots of wine was drunk by the other women, but Fee stuck to ginger ale. She sent me a few pictures of some of the gifts she received. The piles of lace and satin in a rainbow of colors made me grin widely, imagining her modeling them for me. The thought of peeling them off her smooth skin was like a gift that kept on giving.

For now, though, I needed my bride.

We were in a beautiful ballroom overlooking Toronto. The space was decorated with flowers, tulle, flickering candles, and the tables were dressed in cream and green linens. I waited at the altar, complete with a flower-laden arch at one end of the room. Our friends stood around us, waiting to celebrate after the short ceremony with dinner and dancing.

Joanne appeared in the doorway and walked sedately toward us, her gaze lingering on Rene for a long moment. I glanced to the side, noting the wide grin on his face and the way his eyes were focused on her. I had been surprised when I finally met her to discover she was older than Fee by ten years. There had been no disguising the mutual attraction between her and Rene the first time they met, and watching the two of them now made me wonder how far their attraction had gone.

Rene met my amused gaze. "Keep your eyes on your own woman," he growled softly.

I chuckled. "Is that how it is, old man?"

He nudged me playfully. "None of your business, Halton. You concentrate on getting married. I'll handle my own love life."

My laughter died on my lips when Fee appeared in the doorway. The short path to me seemed much too long as I watched her walk my way.

Her beautiful silver hair was down, hanging past her shoulders in a mass of waves, shining in the low light. A lacy, ivory dress gathered tight under her breasts and swirled loosely around her knees, a vivid green sash emphasizing the baby bump she was proud to display.

Lord knew I could hardly keep my hands off of it. Every time she was close, I found myself touching it. Sitting beside her, I always rested my hand on the growing swell. I talked to her tummy endlessly at night while she slept. I kissed it constantly, murmuring my adoration to her skin. I sang funny songs, ignoring Fee's snickers, and I read books about foxes, puppies, and kittens to the growing bump daily.

Any and all doubts I would love this child, *our child*, were banished instantly when I saw the first ultrasound. I was already in love, but seeing the image had kicked my emotions into overload, and now I was totally infatuated. We didn't know the gender, but it didn't matter. My child already owned my heart.

Our eyes met, intense dark blue melding with soft, beautiful green, and my heart stuttered. This was the woman I would spend the rest of my life with. This was the woman who would safeguard my heart and always be there. And I would do the same for her.

I held out my hand, anxious to feel her touch. Her smile was wide, her eyes joyful as she slid her palm into mine, and I lifted our joined fingers to my mouth, kissing her knuckles.

"Ready, FeeNelly?" I asked quietly.

"So ready, counselor."

"Then let's get married."

Four years later

I pulled in the driveway, pausing before hurrying up the steps to admire the lines of the new house. Much larger than the house Fee and I shared when we were first married, this one had five bedrooms and a good-sized yard, complete with a pool. The house was farther outside of Toronto than I ever expected to live, but it was in a good, safe neighborhood for my family. I had opened a second office closer to the new house and spent two days a week in Toronto and the other three in the new one so I was nearer to home. Both offices were busy and productive. Rene still ran the Toronto office, and Clark now ran the second place.

I glanced at my watch, hoping I wasn't late. I tapped in the combination code for the door and went inside, to be greeted by one of my favorite sounds in the world.

My daughter, Elsie Renee, bounded down the steps, squealing my name. I opened my arms and caught her as she flung herself off the bottom stair. I swung her around, laughing at her delighted squeaks, then gathered her close and kissed her head. She smelled of bubble bath, flowers, and little girl. She clutched a cookie in her hand and offered it to me with a flourish.

"Is that for me?"

She squirmed in my arms, her grin wide. "Mommy and me made them!"

I studied the cookie, noting the little nibbles missing on one part.

"I think a little mouse ate my cookie."

She giggled and leaned up, her little lips at my ear. "Not a mouse, Daddy. It was me!"

I opened my eyes wide, lifting my eyebrows in fake surprise. "I never would have guessed that."

She giggled, and I bit into the dense cookie, enjoying the chocolate.

"Where is Mommy?"

"Upstairs. I was waiting for you." She met my eyes, her green irises so like Fee's. She had my dark hair, but other than that, she was Fee all over, including her tiny stature. "I missed you!"

I rubbed her nose playfully with mine. "I missed you, baby girl."

She leaned forward, pressing our foreheads together, her voice low as if she was telling me a secret. "I needs a story, Daddy."

I tossed the rest of the cookie into my mouth, settled her on my hip, and headed up the stairs. "Then you get one."

I paused in the door of the nursery, gazing at the sweet sight. Fee was in her rocking chair, our new son nuzzling at her breast.

"Hey, FeeNelly."

Her luminous eyes were bright as she beamed at me. "Hey yourself, counselor."

I strolled to the rocking chair and bent, dropping a kiss to her full mouth, then bending farther down to press my lips to my son's head. Elsie, as usual, had to get in on the action and dropped about a hundred kisses on Brandon's head.

I stood and cupped Fee's cheek. "Everything okay? You look tired, love."

"He was a little fussy today. I think he missed his daddy."

I ran my finger over his downy cheek. "I missed him."

I had taken two weeks off when Brandon was born and, for the first time in my life, had dreaded returning to work. I was busy and productive all day, but my thoughts often strayed to where my heart was—back home with my family.

"We'll figure it out," she assured me.

"I was thinking of going to a four-day week. Two downtown, two here, and one at home." I lifted Elsie, settling her head into the crook of my neck as I rubbed her back in long passes, knowing how much she loved it when I did that. She sighed and snuggled closer in contentment.

Fee's expression turned joyful. I loved seeing her look at me that way.

"I'd like that."

"I'm also thinking of hiring another lawyer and cutting back more over the next year."

Fee stroked Brandon's head as she regarded me. "Don't make a decision based on one day back at work, Halton. Your emotions are talking right now."

"And I'm listening. I denied them too long." I sighed and pressed a kiss to Elsie's head. "I don't want to miss their childhood. Rene pointed out that I could start taking more of an advisory approach. Sit in on meetings, help direct the cases, but not work on them. Let the others handle that part and free up a lot of my time. Do three days and be home for the rest."

"We'd like that. All of us."

Our gazes locked, and a silent conversation passed between us.

My eyes pleaded with her to understand my need to be with her and our kids as much as possible. Her green gaze was gentle and compassionate. She gave me an imperceptible nod, letting me know she would support me no matter what I decided.

Elsie lifted her head, tapping my cheek to get my attention. "Story, Daddy."

"Right." I lowered her to Fee's level. "Kiss Mommy goodnight."

Once the kiss-fest was done, I carried Elsie across the hall to her room. Pinks, purples, and yellow reigned supreme in there. Lace, frills, and stuffed toys abounded. It was as girly as it could be. I settled into the large chair in the corner after tossing aside a dozen stuffed toys and tucked Elsie onto my lap. Her new "big girl" bed was way too small for me to be comfortable on, and I knew by experience, story time was at least thirty minutes. Elsie had inherited one other thing from me—my restlessness at night. We found keeping her to a routine helped. A warm bath, a story, and being held close helped settle her, and once she fell asleep, she rarely woke up these days. I had to admit it was my favorite time of day.

I glanced at the overflowing bookshelf. "What one, baby girl?"

"A daddy story."

"Ah." She liked it when I made up stories and told them to her. She also liked funny voices and lots of princesses. They were often the same basic story, but I always threw in something new. Fee assured me it was the tone of my voice and my closeness that Elsie liked the most.

I pursed my lips.

"Once upon a time, there was a princess named Fee."

"Like Mommy!"

I kissed her head. "Yep."

"One day, the princess went for a walk and got lost. She kept walking and looking for a friend to help her. Deep in the forest, she met a mean monster. He lived alone in a cave."

I heard Fee's gentle laughter drift across the hall.

"Was she scared?"

243

"Nope. The princess was brave, and she knew the monster wouldn't hurt her. She was smart like that."

Elsie furrowed her little brow, looking so much like Fee, I had to kiss her nose.

"Did he have a name, Daddy?"

"Yes. His name was Smitty."

Fee laughed again, and I leaned back, peering across the hall. Her head rested against the back of the rocking chair, and she was watching us. She had set up the rooms so she could easily see both children from each chair, and it came in handy at night. I threw her a wink, and she shook her head.

"Why was Smitty alone?"

"He was snarly and growly."

"How come?"

I stroked Elsie's downy cheek. "He had a thorn in his paw nobody knew about. It hurt him all the time."

Her eyes grew round. "Like a boo-boo?"

"Yes."

"He didn't have a mommy to kiss it better?"

"Nope. He was a grown-up monster."

She frowned. "That is sad."

I chuckled. "The princess told Smitty she was lost and needed his help. He said no, but she asked again and smiled at him. Smitty thought it was the most beautiful smile he had ever seen, so he said okay. He showed the princess how to get home, but before she could thank him, he walked away. But the princess remembered his kindness. A few days later, the princess was out for a walk again and ran into the monster. She tried to talk to him, but he was rude."

Fee's voice floated between the rooms. "He was egotistical too."

I never raised my voice, although I tried not to laugh. I met her gaze again, trying to look stern. "Enough from the peanut gallery."

She lifted Brandon to her shoulder, rocking and patting his back. I loved seeing her with our children. It made me warm inside.

Little fingers pulled at my beard. "What happened, Daddy?"

"Princess Fee was a magical princess. She had long silver hair that hid her magic wand, and when Smitty walked away from her, she waved it in the air, and it showed her the thorn that was deep in his skin."

"And?" she asked anxiously.

"Princess Fee followed Smitty home and used her wand to make the thorn disappear."

Elsie clapped her hands. "Then he wasn't grumpy?"

"Nope. In fact, as soon as the thorn disappeared, Smitty turned into the most handsome prince in the world. He was charming and smooth, and Princess Fee fell in love with him. She waved her magic wand again and turned his cave into a palace."

"Yay!"

Fee's snicker was louder this time, and I turned to see her leaning against the doorjamb.

"Charming and smooth?" she challenged.

"Very charming. The princess couldn't resist."

"Uh-huh."

Elsie tapped my cheek to get my attention. "What then?"

"The prince married the princess, and they lived happily ever after."

Elsie sighed, leaning her head against my shoulder. "Good story, Daddy."

Fee pushed off the frame. "Well, at least you got that part right."

I watched her walk away, holding my son.

My daughter snuggled closer, her little body growing heavy as she fell asleep. I always knew when she was out because she made the same noise Fee did when she slept, although Elsie's was more clicking than purring. I now had two raptors in the house—and I loved every minute of it.

I looked around the room and listened to the sounds of my family settling for the night—my daughter's little clicking, Fee's voice gently crooning to Brandon, and his coo as he fell asleep.

Once they were settled, I could spend the rest of the evening with my beautiful wife and catch up on all the things I missed during the day. Catch up with her.

Then I would find the peaceful rest only she could give me.

My Fee.

I had everything I had ever dreamed of and was too afraid to hope for.

A real home, a family I adored—all because of the woman who proved to me that love didn't always come with pain. Who was strong enough to show me that every day.

She created a whole new world for me, and I gave her the one she deserved.

One filled with unending love.

That was us. Our story—our forever.

Our happily ever after.

ACKNOWLEDGMENTS

~Thank you ~
As always, I have some people to thank. The ones behind the words
that encourage and support. The people who make these books
possible for so many reasons.

To my readers—thank you for taking a chance on this series.
Your love of BAM makes me so happy!

Lisa, thank you for your editing brilliance and patience.
I love reading your comments and knowing I make you laugh.

Beth, Trina, Melissa—thank you for your feedback and support.

Carrie, my UN ladies, Ayden, Jeannie, Freya—
I love you and am honored to call you friends. You humble me.

Peggy and Deb, thank you for your support and keen eyes.

Melissa—you take my scatterbrained ideas and turn them into covers
I adore. Thank you!

Karen, my dear friend and PA. There are simply not enough words.
What you do cannot be described, and the gratitude I feel cannot be
expressed. Much love.

To all the bloggers, readers, and especially my review team. Thank
you for everything you do. Shouting your love of books—of my work

—posting, sharing—your recommendations keep my TBR list full, and the support you have shown me is so appreciated.

To my fellow authors who have shown me such kindness, thank you. I will follow your example and pay it forward.

My reader group, Melanie's Minions—love you all.

And My Matthew. Love isn't a big enough word. One lifetime isn't enough. Yours forever. Always.

BOOKS BY

Vested Interest Series

Bentley (Vested Interest #1)

Aiden (Vested Interest #2)

Maddox (Vested Interest #3)

Reid (Vested Interest #4)

Van (Vested Interest #5)

Insta-Spark Collection

It Started with a Kiss

Christmas Sugar

An Instant Connection

The Contract Series

The Contract

The Baby Clause (Contract #2)

Standalones

Into the Storm

Beneath the Scars

Over the Fence

My Image of You (Random House/Loveswept)

ABOUT THE AUTHOR

New York Times/USA Today bestselling author Melanie Moreland, lives a happy and content life in a quiet area of Ontario with her beloved husband of thirty plus years and their rescue cat, Amber. Nothing means more to her than her friends and family, and she cherishes every moment spent with them.

While seriously addicted to coffee, and highly challenged with all things computer-related and technical, she relishes baking, cooking, and trying new recipes for people to sample. She loves to throw dinner parties, and enjoys traveling, here and abroad, but finds coming home is always the best part of any trip.

Melanie loves stories, especially paired with a good wine, and enjoys skydiving (free falling over a fleck of dust) extreme snowboarding (falling down stairs) and piloting her own helicopter (tripping over her own feet). She's learned happily ever afters, even bumpy ones, are all in how you tell the story.

Melanie is represented by Flavia Viotti at Bookcase Literary Agency. For any questions regarding subsidiary or translation rights please contact her at flavia@bookcaseagency.com

Connect with Melanie

Like reader groups? Lots of fun and giveaways! Check it out Melanie Moreland's Minions

Join my newsletter for up-to-date news, sales, book announcements and excerpts (no spam): Melanie Moreland's newsletter

Visit my website www.melaniemoreland.com

CPSIA information can be obtained
at www.ICGtesting.com
Printed in the USA
LVHW082203300619
622820LV00027B/636/P